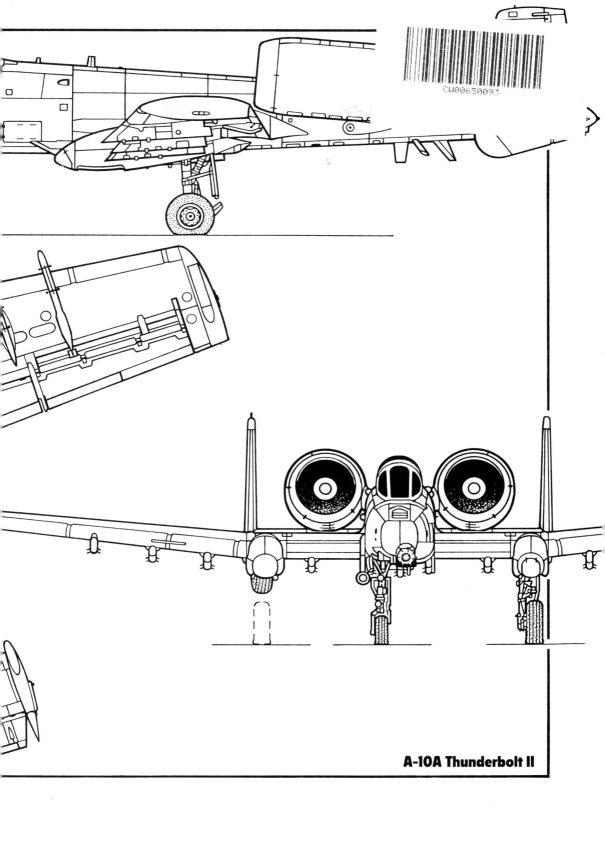

A-10A Thunderbolt II

A-10
THUNDERBOLT II

Modern Combat Aircraft 28

A-10 THUNDERBOLT II

Mike Spick

LONDON
IAN ALLAN LTD

First published 1987

ISBN 0 7110 1747 6

Published by Ian Allan Ltd, Shepperton, Surrey; and printed by Ian Allan Printing Ltd at their works at Coombelands in Runnymede, England

Front cover:
A sharkmouthed A-10A of the 23rd TFW. Note the open refuelling point on the left gear nacelle. *Frank Mormillo*

Back cover, top:
A 354th TFW Warthog lets it all hang out as it turns into the circuit at the end of an arduous training mission. *Peter Foster*

Centre:
The countershaded two-tone grey finish was used by the 354th TFW into 1980. Here unit A-10s are shown deployed to Indian Springs Air Force Auxiliary Field. *Frank Mormillo*

Bottom:
The Warthog lends itself to caricature. *Mike Ryan*

Contents

United States distribution by

Publishers & Wholesalers Inc
Osceola, Wisconsin 54020, USA ®

Acknowledgements

The Warthog only ever saw service in one variant, has never fired a shot in anger, and has been out of production for some considerable time. It is also likely to be phased out of front line service in its primary role by the end of the decade. These factors have compounded the difficulties of saying anything new about it, and I am therefore grateful for the assistance that I have received from both the manufacturers and the United States Air Force. In particular, I should like to thank the following:

Mr Thomas Turner of Fairchild Industries; Kent Schubert and Dwight Weber of General Electric; Arthur J. Wallis representing Hughes; and my good friend Dr Alfred Price, who provided some original material from his archives. On the military side, thanks are due to Capt Leslie Fraze of 3rd Air Force; Maj Joe L. Hodges; Lt-Col Robert J. Burke, the Assistant Deputy Commander of Operations at RAF Bentwaters/Woodbridge; Capt Mike Ryan, Tech Sgt Bruce Christopherson and Sgt John Bylack of the 81st TFW. From the other side of the Atlantic, material was provided by Capt Guy C. Thompson of 23rd TFW, 2nd Lt Eugene E. Ehlers of 128th TFW; S/Sgt Jesse C. Edmiston of 434th TFW; M/Sgt Richard A. Curry of 917th TFG; and S/Sgt Bradley S. Kadrich of 354th TFW.

Prologue

The concept of giving aerial support to the ground forces is hardly new: it has been practised widely since 1917. It involved hanging bombs on whatever fighter aircraft could be spared at the time and sending them out to strafe the enemy. During World War 2, a few specialised close air support types appeared, notably the Ju-87 Stuka, the Hs 129 tankbuster, and the Il-2. These were successful where a measure of local air superiority could be obtained, but were very vulnerable to enemy fighters where it could not. Weighed down by protective armour, they were slower and less manoeuvrable than their opponents, and could be easily caught, outflown and shot down. On the other hand the anti-aircraft guns of the day were also formidable adversaries, and the armour which weighed them down in air combat was invaluable in protecting them when carrying out their primary mission. To summarise, when flying the close air support mission, fighters might or might not be encountered, but ground fire always would. The armour also gave a measure of protection against the guns of fighters; while its weight made the attack aircraft easier to hit, it also made it harder to shoot down. But this notwithstanding, the majority of close air support missions in World War 2 were flown by fighters carrying air-to-ground munitions: Typhoons with rockets, P-47s with bombs, etc.

The first widespread use of jet fighters occurred in the Korean War of 1950-53. The vast majority of the missions flown were air-to-ground, many of them by fast jets, but piston-engined types such as the A-26 Intruder and the A-1 Skyraider proved very effective. While they were easily outperformed by the opposing MiG-15 fighters, they operated in the main beneath a protective umbrella of F-86 Sabres, which succeeded in almost entirely divorcing the air superiority battle from the air/land battle going on below. This meant that the attack aircraft could concentrate on their work without having to worry overmuch about enemy fighters intervening, which created another artificial aspect to the air war, the result of which was that no firm conclusions could be drawn from it for future application.

The technology explosion of the 1950s saw fighter speeds double and treble, and ceilings increase greatly. Speed and height were seen as the keys both to mission success, and to survival. Clever missiles — both air-to-air and air-to-ground

— with a theoretically very high P_k (kill probability) — were expected to supplant the short ranged gun as the main aircraft and counter-aircraft weapon. The 'worst case' scenario was always a full-scale war in Central Europe, with the widespread use of tactical nuclear weapons. The close air support mission concept fell into decline, with the new breed of fighter-bombers such as the Mach 2-capable F-105 Thunderchief leading the way to the future. Then came the Vietnam War.

The Vietnam War was like no other and, despite its title, spread into the adjoining countries of Cambodia and Laos, and to a lesser degree Thailand. It was fought over terrain which was a mix of jungle, mountain and flat plains; in generally foul weather, with poor visibility, low cloud bases and a monsoon season lasting for months on end; against an enemy who was difficult to locate; and, until he started shooting, was almost as difficult to identify. The air war divided basically into two parts: the air war against North Vietnam, and the in-country war. It is the in-country war that concerns us here, as effectively there were no borders, no front lines. The situation was fluid, in the most total sense. In the morning the attack aircraft might take off and fly north to their targets; in the afternoon they might just as easily fly south; while that night, their airfield could come under mortar attack by an enemy who was nowhere to be seen the following morning.

Interdiction missions were everyday events in the in-country war, and close air support missions almost as frequent when the Viet Cong launched one of their surprise strikes, or North Vietnamese regulars made a cross-border incursion. A high proportion of these missions were flown by fast jets, through lack of anything more suitable. Maj Joe L. Hodges flew the F-100D Super Sabre in the theatre from mid-1970 to mid-1971, clocking up a total of 255 missions. The 'Hun', as the F-100 was affectionately known, was a single seat supersonic fighter with a relatively high wing loading, armed with four 20mm revolver cannon. It was short ranged for the task, and could carry a moderate load of air-to-ground munitions externally. It carried no automatic weapons delivery systems, but was a stable platform. Maj Hodges' recollections highlight some of the problems of flying the close air support mission in a fast jet:

'Basically there was no air threat, and the ground defences were mainly small arms and a few quadruple 20mm guns. Just occasionally you'd run across a 37mm triple A. When I arrived there were no SAMs, but by the time I left there were. If possible we would stay above the range of the small arms fire, but sometimes we had to go down into it, depending on what the target was and what we were carrying. They could put up a lot of lead with small arms. Some guys tried to avoid small arms fire by using a curvilinear approach, only rolling out to aim in the last couple of seconds. This was OK if you could keep the target in sight during the approach, but often you couldn't. Often we had to dive-bomb, and I remember diving through the flak on some of my early missions. I might be No 3 in the flight, and this is not a good place to be. The leader would go in and you could see the little white puffs of the 20mm AAA all round him. No 2 goes in, more puffs; then it's your turn, you feel a little nervous diving through that stuff, although the chances of being hit are not high. I guess the most hazardous ones are those you don't see. I was flying No 2 to our Wing Commander one time. He rolled in and dropped, then just as I was getting ready to roll in, they shot 37mm at me, five or six shots all at once. I never saw it, but both my leader and the Forward Air Controller (FAC) saw it and said get out of there. It caught me right at the slowest part of the roll-in while I was busy watching the speed on the airplane. They had just watched my leader roll in from the same position. I didn't get hit; in fact, in all my time in South-East Asia I was never hit once.'

From the above it can be seen that one of the disadvantages of a fast jet in this type of mission is keeping the target in sight. A slower aircraft mig[ht] be able to use terrain masking, acquiring t[he] target, then approaching under cover; but brea[k]ing out to aim and release the weapons at the la[st] moment was not possible. For a start, no stand-o[ff] weapons were carried. At attack speeds, the lar[ge] turning radius of the highly wing loaded Hun w[as] too great to allow much 'fine tuning' of the ai[m] point; the Hun had to be pointed pretty accurate[ly] from the outset and the target never lost sight o[f]. This required height, from which the fighter cou[ld] be seen coming. Generally it was a small numbe[r] engagement, with little confusion factor to ups[et] the defenders. Finally, you could never be sure [of] what you were up against. For accuracy you had [to] release from within range of the 20mm but cou[ld] stay outside the small arms envelope — but, as w[e] have just seen, if the defences started chuckin[g] 37mm bricks, it became a different ball gam[e]. Also, defensive fire was not the only hazard.

'During the time I was there, my squadron lo[st] three or four guys, and during my last six mont[hs] the wing (four squadrons) lost about one a mont[h]. Half the time we didn't know whether it w[as] ground fire or what. They just went out and didn['t] come back. Sometimes we would do a low lev[el] guns pass, it was easy to get target fixation and h[it] the trees. You can haul the nose up quick enoug[h] but it takes a little while before the airplane star[ts] to go the way it's pointed. Sometimes that's to[o] late. On one occasion my airplane picked up [a] chunk of timber the size of your fist. We we[re] supporting troops moving up the side of [a] mountain, bombing into the hillside, and I think [I] got too close to the guy in front. I was pretty low [as] I cleared the ridge. We also had our share [of] accidents. Our Huns were getting pretty old b[y] then. One guy had engine trouble shortly aft[er] take-off, climbing out north from Phan Rang. H[e] tried to recover to Pleiku, which had a sho[rt] runway. He got the airplane on the ground O[K] but couldn't stop. He attempted to eject but w[as] killed.'

Two more points emerge here. High speed reduc[es] the time available for a safe break from a gu[n] pass, and increases the kinetic energy, whi[ch] makes it more difficult to alter the aircraft veloc[ity] vector quickly; much more momentum has to b[e] overcome. Secondly, a single-engined aircraft wi[th] a poor short field performance is more at risk tha[n] a twin with good short field performance. Als[o if he] had the lump of wood FODded Maj Hodg[e's] single engine, he probably would not be around [to] tell the tale. It was a near thing.

'Our usual method of weapons delivery w[as] dive-bombing. Usually we would arrive in th[e] target area at about 12,000ft, contact the FAC a[nd]

6

e would tell us what he wanted us to do. The afest way to get the dive angle right was to fly longside the target, and get the right amount of ateral offset so that when you are looking over our shoulder and down you are looking right at it. hen you'd make a 90 degree turn and push over ato the dive. The usual angle was between 35 and 5 degrees. Occasionally you might go straight own; there were all sorts of ways of doing it. Iormally we released the munitions at about ,000ft, but sometimes we did daisycutters, a hallow angle dive to almost ground level. You ull off target and look back over your shoulder to ee how the bombs hit. Generally accuracy was retty good. I remember once I was tasked with itting a French-style colonial house up in the aountains where we had word the Viet Cong were oled up. The plan was that I hit the front of the ouse with napalm to flush the Cong out the back, hile two more of the flight made a low guns pass n the back to catch them coming out. As I rolled a from around 12,000ft, I just felt it was one of ose days when everything was perfect. The ouse had a big portico, with a black and white, robably marble, tiled floor, and I took this as my ming point. I dropped, and pulled up, and would ou believe, the nape went straight in through the ont door. All the other guys saw coming out back as flames! The strike picture showed it perfectly.'

Vith no automated weapons delivery system, ombing accuracy was very much a matter of 'by

guess and by god', with plenty of Kentucky windage thrown in. The release, at about 4,000ft altitude, was to allow a pull-out above the effective range of small arms fire, and to avoid the 20mm AAA having too much in range time in which to adjust their aim.

'We carried two sorts of loads: soft loads, made up of nape and high drag bombs, and hard loads, which were slicks (low drag bombs). We had a mix of loads available at the pads so we could get off quickly once a target was identified. The slick was not really a close air support weapon, it's more for interdiction. It had to be released from a higher altitude, and the accuracy was often not as good. Just occasionally we carried CBUs (cluster bombs). These were for an area attack. They had to be released at just the right height to get the pattern; release too low and they were concentrated in a small area, too high and they would do-nut, form a ring with a hole in the centre, the hole being where your aim point was. If the target was suitable, we strafed with our 20mm cannon. We used high explosive incendiary. You could see the flashes where they hit; sometimes you would get secondary explosions'.

Apart from the inherent limitations of a fast jet in hitting small point targets, the weaponry did not lend itself to extreme accuracy of attack, but the four 20mm cannon, which did, involved getting very low down, well into the range of small arms return fire. Stand-off weapons would have been much more satisfactory, but they were not available at this time to this unit. Maj Hodges continues on the subject of accuracy.

'When you have a target you could see, like a building, or vehicles, or sometimes we attacked sampans on the Mekong River, then that was an aid to accuracy. But of my 255 missions, on 50 or so I never saw a target. I just dropped the loads on

Right:
The old and the new: Ultrahog and
Warthog line up together. An
A-10A awaiting delivery to the 81st
TFW finds itself next to a previous
Fairchild Republic product, an
F-105 Thunderchief of the Virginia
Air National Guard. *Fairchild*

Below:
Close Air Support: Although
skylined for the photographer, if
this Warthog was rolling in at a
target it would probably be below
the horizon for the attack run, and
therefore less visible. *Fairchild*

Below right:
A spectacular piece of terrain
following takes this A-10A
undetected to its target. Flying the
Warthog certainly has some
compensations.
Fairchild via A. Thornborough

FAC's instructions. When the target was hidden b
jungle, it was often difficult to pick up, even witl
FAC's guidance.

'It surprised me a bit to find that there was a fai
amount of night work. This was generally ir
support of isolated special forces groups. Normall
we went out in twos, equipped with flares. On
would light up the area with flares while the othe
attacked, then switch roles. Sometimes w

We'd go up there, and contact a FAC on the ground. He had a sort of flare which only gave a point light source, and he'd set it up, it might be on a mountain top, or down in the bottom of a valley, and tell us where to aim in relation to it. A point light source is real tough to bomb. I'll never forget the first time I rolled in. I just worked out the side like in daylight, and did what I thought was a typical roll in, pulled my nose around and put my sight on this point of light. I looked back into the office to check my dive angle, expecting to see between 30 and 45 degrees. *I was in a 60 degree dive!* It was really exciting; it was completely black outside the cockpit, with no visual references at all. We went out there three nights in a row, and got used to it a bit.'

The lesson here is simple. Every military aircraft will, in a war situation, be used for something which was never envisaged at the design stage. The war does not stop at sunset, and there are never enough specialist night birds to go round. Nor are there ever enough aircraft for them always to be in the right place at the right time, as the next excerpt shows.

'My unit, the 35th Tactical Fighter Wing, was based at Phan Rang. Sometimes we had to go a long way west, into the Mekong delta, other times right up into Laos. There was a lot of activity up there. One time we had to support ground forces up at Than Hai; it was 350 miles up there, and we hadn't got the range. After the attack we had to land at Ubon, in Thailand, to refuel. We were sent because all the local air power had been used up. One of the big shows was Lam Son 719,

perated under radar control at night, level ropping from high altitude. Other times there /ould be a FAC up on the Ho Chi Minh Trail, and hen we'd be dive-bombing without flares. If you ut flares down, it lights up the ground, not exactly ke daytime, but you have the same sort of visual eferences to get yourself up out of there. Now this articular mission, which we only did for two to hree weeks in December 1970, was different.

codenamed 'Ground Ship Home', in early 1971. That was about the most air power I'd ever seen in one place at one time. We flew out of Phan Rang, went up there and dropped our bombs; came back into Phu Cat, about 50 miles north of Phan Rang to reload, back up to attack, and then recover home. It was a really fierce ground battle: by about Day 4, the NVN army had put about 15,000 troops in up there. Because we were going such a long distance, we frequently arrived at 20,000ft. This was to conserve fuel. Most people were used to bombing from 12,000ft, so they would go down and level off there for the attack. As we had such a long way to go home, it was easier to roll in from 20,000ft, go straight down and come straight back up. This meant that our dive angle was steeper and our weapon release speeds were higher than normal.'

The preceding passage highlights the need for forward basing to give rapid reaction times; it also shows up the unsuitability of the fast jet for this type of work, being too thirsty at lower altitudes to come in at the optimum attack height, when operating over great distances. No comment was made on accuracy when attacking from the greater than normal altitude. Often the enemy were in hardened positions, and often in far closer proximity to the fighter bases.

'About 30 to 40 miles south of Phan Rang was a great granite mountain, with caves, which the NVN used. I don't know how many bombs we dropped on that, to no effect. We tried nape, but it didn't work; it doesn't burn very long. Right at the top was a huge boulder, and someone said if we could loosen that, it would bring half the mountain down and bury the caves. We dropped lots of bombs to try and release this big rock, but it never moved!'

Speed of reaction was essential, both to help hard-pressed 'crunchies' quickly, or to catch a target while it was vulnerable.

'We would scramble off the pad, and copy a vector while in the airplane taxying out. The controller would give us a bearing and distance, and if a FAC was available, a frequency (radio) to work. One day I and another guy scrambled and went out over Cambodia. An earlier air strike had caught a North Vietnamese convoy passing through a town; they had hit the head of it and stopped it. When we got there, there was about 30 vehicles lined up, and troops deployed on both sides of the road ready to shoot back at us. There is a temple in all Cambodian villages, and being a religious building, it was strictly off limits to us. Of course, the bad guys knew this, and that's where they set up their machine guns and stuff; they'd be shooting at us from the temple, and we couldn't shoot back. To fly down the line of the convoy, we had to fly right past the temple, and it was pretty close range stuff. Because of the ground fire, we ran in from opposite directions at the same time to confuse the gunners a bit. We dropped our load, which was bombs and napalm, then came back in for a strafing run. The vehicles had fuel in them so they burned. Two to three weeks later we got a report back on the number of vehicles destroyed and the body count. This was a very successful mission, but also very hazardous for us.'

Below:
An A-10A of the 57th FWW (now the 57th Tactical Training Wing), seen over Nellis AFB in July 1985. *Frank Mormillo*

Above right:
A 104th TFG A-10 deploys its decelerons during a landing roll in December 1980. *Frank Mormillo*

While in this instance neither Hun was hit, it underlines the need for a survivable aircraft when operating in close proximity to enemy fire. Success was due to the speed of reaction, which enabled the American fighters to reach the convoy before the road ahead had been cleared, catching the convoy still stationary in the open.

Finally, Maj Hodges talks about a specific close air support mission.

'The Mekong River runs straight down through Cambodia, then, southwest of a big provincial capital called Kompong Thom, it turns 90 degrees west. Right where it turns, there is a little village called Phe Do Tong. Right in the middle is a crossroads, with the roads running north to south and east to west. A whole NVN army division had come down from the north, and were opposed by about a company of Cambodians, who had holed up in a schoolhouse in the southeast quarter, about half a mile south of the intersection. There was also a temple in the same quarter which was used for air defence guns by the NVN, who occupied a lot of individual buildings around the schoolhouse. We supported them day and night for five days; after which the NVN backed off, leaving the Cambodians still in the schoolhouse. Our accuracy had to be pretty high, as the troops were in close contact, and we had to get in close to be sure of our aim. This involved a higher level of risk to the aircrew, but the circumstances were such that it had to be done.'

This is a striking example of the effectiveness of air power, although it seems probable that the NVN strength was more like a battalion than a division. To enable a badly outnumbered Cambodian company to hold out for five days in the face of overwhelming odds was no mean feat, and to force the attackers to retire was even more remarkable, indicating a high level of accuracy.

While the preceding extracts show that the fast jets of the 35th TFW did a very fair job, it should be remembered that most of the missions were flown in fair weather which allowed targets to be identified from 12,000ft or higher. A low cloud base, especially in mountainous country, would have precluded the use of the Super Sabre completely, as it was too fast to pick up a target and attack from low level in a single pass, while at attack speeds its turn radius was too large to allow it to keep the target in sight while remaining at low level, in poor visibility. If operating in a valley, it could in most cases not even get round in the available space. This limited it basically to dive-bombing attacks, lining up in full view of the enemy air defences and giving them plenty of time to aim. Had the ground-to-air defences been stronger this could have been disastrous. Nor were stand-off, precision-guided munitions available to the unit. A really accurate attack meant getting in close, and running the gauntlet of the defences. The Hun had virtually no loiter capability, and rapid response was only achieved by a quick scramble off the pad. Nor was forward basing on semi-prepared strips possible: the Hun had poor short field performance. Clearly something more suited to the task was needed. At the time of Maj Hodges' tour of operations, this had been recognised. Two other types were widely used for the CAS mission in Vietnam: the Cessna A-37 Dragonfly, and the Douglas A-1 Skyraider. The A-37 was a jet trainer developed for light attack and counter-insurgency missions, while the A-1 was a propeller-driven dive-bomber developed from a World War 2 specification. Of these, the A-1 was by far the most suitable for the task: it could carry heavy loads for long distances, it had exceptional endurance, it was agile enough to operate down under the weather, had the right speed range for the job, good short field performance, and was rugged, able to take a beating and still get back to base. The main problem was that production had ceased many years before. A new design, optimised for the role, was needed.

2 Concept & Development

The A-10A Thunderbolt II is an optimised close air support machine with a distinct bias towards tank-busting, designed to operate in a worst case Central European scenario. It has other possible applications, but so has everything else that flies. Its origins lie far back in the 1960s, in the South-East Asia theatre, when Gen John P. Mc-Connell, the then USAF Chief of Staff, visited the area, and made a close examination of the air war requirements. He concluded that the requirements of the CAS mission varied considerably from those of the interdiction mission. The American definition of CAS is: 'air attacks against hostile targets which are in close proximity to friendly forces, and which require detailed integration of each air mission with the fire and movement of those forces'. Interdiction, on the other hand, is a mission generally carried out behind the enemy lines, often involving a deep penetration of hostile air space, where the proximity of friendly ground units, with the attendant risk of collateral damage, is not a factor. A different type of aircraft is required for each mission. Interdiction demands speed, both to lessen the time spent in hostile air space, and to reduce the risk of interception, and a reduction in the accuracy of weapons delivery can be accepted to achieve this. The USAF in 1966, the year of Gen McConnell's visit, had several types of fast jet that could carry out the interdiction mission, and had just ordered the Vought A-7D, an Air Force version of a US Navy attack fighter, to supplement them. This was not the case for the CAS mission, and Gen McConnell suggested that an optimised aircraft be developed.

This proposal, which can be regarded as the origin of the A-10, was to be similar in capability to the A-1 but better all round, and cheaper than the A-7D. It can be surmised that the reference to the A-7D crept in to prevent the new project from being stillborn; had it cost more than the A-7D — which was a very capable machine — political pressure would have been brought to bear to buy more A-7s instead. The initial requirement called for a strong, simple and easy to maintain aircraft

Below:
The first YA-10 prototype lifts off from Edwards AFB. The gun is a 20mm M61A, and the underfuselage strakes have yet to be added. *Fairchild*

Above right:
The much sleeker Northrop YA-9 lifts off, accompanied by a T-37 chase plane, the attack version of which was used for the CAS mission in South Vietnam. *Northrop*

Right:
The fuselage shell moves along the production line, showing the huge amount of space needed to house the monster cannon. *Fairchild*

with a high level of agility, a long loiter time, able to operate from semi-prepared strips close to the fighting, with a heavy weapons load. On 6 March 1967 the requirement became official with the issue of a Request For Proposals (RFP) for design studies of a new low-cost attack aircraft under the designation A-X (attack experimental), to no less than 21 aircraft manufacturers. The RFP was itself non-specific; it had to produce an aircraft that was faster than the Skyraider, with at least similar endurance and weapons loads, and be more survivable.

The next step came quickly; on 2 May of that year contracts were awarded for preliminary design and other studies, including survivability, to just four companies. These were General Dynamics, Grumman, Northrop and McDonnell Douglas. Meanwhile, as the North Vietnamese Army stepped up its efforts using conventional forces, replacing the guerilla attacks of the Viet Cong to a large degree, the need to knock out tanks became evident. The gun was obviously an excellent weapon for the CAS mission, used for accurate strafing in close proximity to friendly forces; a gun suitable for knocking out tanks was now added to the list of studies.

This was further reinforced by the experience of the Israeli Air Force in the Six Day War of June 1967, when its Mystere IVs and Ouragans succeeded in knocking out a considerable number of Russian-built tanks with their 30mm DEFA cannon. The frontal armour of a main battle tank is nigh on impenetrable by the ordinary aircraft cannon, even with armour-piercing ammunition, but it is thinner at the sides, and even more vulnerable from the rear — especially the engine covers — and on the top. The mobility of an aircraft enables it to work around for the rear attack with ease.

Another factor enters the equation here. The usual picture of a tank being knocked out shows an interior explosion and bits flying off; it is all very

13

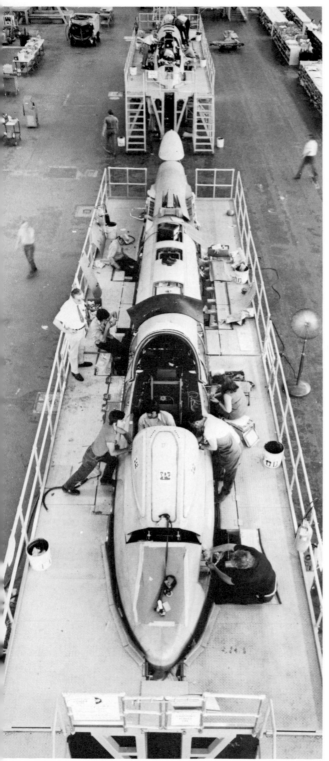

spectacular and bloodthirsty. In practice there are other ways of taking out a tank. The immobilisation hit can be pretty effective in slowing the impetus of a tank attack; and knocking a track off, with one of the bogies for good measure, effectively removes the tank from an attacking force, while jamming the turret is even better. The turret ring was stated to be one of the primary aiming points for Israeli Ouragan pilots. As the standard 20mm shell used by the American services was not up to the job, development of an optimised tank-busting gun was quietly started, and built into the general requirements. The new gun would have to be large and powerful; but it would be too big to be fitted into an existing design; therefore the aircraft would have to be designed around it. It had gradually become a flying gun rather than a munitions hauler.

Just over three years from the original RFP, the definitive RFP was issued, on 7 May 1970, to a total of 12 manufacturers for the development of competitive prototypes, with a submission date of 10 August that year. Adverse weather operations were emphasised; the A-X had to be manoeuvrable enough to be effective beneath a 1,000ft ceiling, with horizontal visibility of 1nm (one nautical mile). A warload of 9,500lb had to be carried a distance of 250nm, followed by two hours loiter, then return to base with a 30min fuel margin. Convoy escort radius was the same, while reconnaissance, flown without external weapons or fuel, was to be 100nm further. Ferry range against a 50kt headwind was to be 2,300nm. The manoeuvre requirements were stated in terms of the load factor; sustained turns of 2.2g at a true air speed of 150kt, and 3.5g at 275kt were called for, and a 5g instantaneous turn at 300kt. In round figures, the respective turn radii are 975ft, 2,000ft, and 1,600ft, while the rates of turn in degrees per second are 15, 13½, and 18. These figures would allow an about face of 180° to be made in well under 15 seconds, with a minimal penetration of defended air space, far better than any fast jet could achieve. In practice an A-10A laden with six 500lb bombs in 'hot and high' conditions was later to achieve 5.8g instantaneous. Maximum sea level speed was to be 400kt, reducing to 350kt at 5,000ft with six Mk 82 bombs. The stabilised dive speed at angles up to 45° was to be 260kt calibrated air

speed, while at maximum weight the take-off and landing distance should not exceed 4,000ft, reducing to 1,000ft at forward operating weight. It is relevant that hardly any aircraft operates at anywhere near its maximum weight.

Two other factors were stressed. At low altitudes and low speed over the battle area, the A-X was going to take hits. It not only had to be able to survive all but the most destructive impacts and still return to base; it had to be easily and quickly repairable, to enable it to be returned to action with the minimum delay. The watchwords were survivability and repairability, the last equating well with the need for maintainability and the final requirement of designing to cost. Two competing proposals would be chosen and two development prototypes of each would be funded. These would then participate in a fly-off to determine the most suitable design, which after further evaluation would be selected by the Air Force.

Also in 1970, a further RFP was issued for the tank-busting gun, to be designated GAU-8. It was to be a 30mm calibre weapon, with a high muzzle velocity, and a rate of fire of 4,000 rounds per minute. Four companies, later narrowed down to Philco-Ford and General Electric, competed for the gun contract, and it was eventually won by the latter company.

Out of the dozen manufacturers that received the A-X RFP in May, exactly half had responded by the time the deadline was reached. They were Boeing Vertol, Cessna, Fairchild's Republic Aviation division, General Dynamics, Lockheed and Northrop. By this time the USAF knew fairly precisely what it wanted, and the preliminary evaluation was swift. Boeing Vertol, a helicopter manufacturer, had submitted the only propeller-driven design, and this was quickly eliminated. On 18 December the result was announced: the two contractors selected to carry their proposals through to the prototype development phase were Fairchild and Northrop. In March 1971 the two proposals received official Air Force designations, the Northrop aircraft becoming the YA-9 and the Fairchild machine the YA-10. Both types were to be designed around the enormous GAU-8 that was in prospect, but as development of the gun was running behind that of the aircraft, all development machines were to be fitted with the 20mm M61 multi-barrel cannon for the trials.

When competing aircraft are built to meet the same operational requirement, it is not unusual for them to come out looking fairly similar. In the A-X competition this was not the case; apart from having two engines and a high aspect ratio wing, the YA-9 and YA-10 had little in common. Northrop produced a large but rather elegant

aircraft with a single fin and high-set tailplane, a shoulder-mounted wing, and mid-set engines faired into the fuselage sides. Fairchild had, by contrast, obviously thrown the old maxim 'if it looks right, it generally is right' out of the window, and produced an unorthodox layout that was once rather unkindly described to me by an F-15 driver as 'looking like a collection of afterthoughts'. In fact, every facet of the design had been considered carefully, and either an optimum or a trade-off solution adopted.

On first seeing an A-10 from close to, the abiding impressions are firstly, what a large aircraft it is, and secondly, how high off the ground it stands. As to the first impression, any aircraft built to contain the GAU-8 could hardly be smaller, while the ground clearance stems from the need to carry ordnance beneath the fuselage, coupled with a wide track main gear for easy handling on rough fields. In order to obtain a wide track for the gear, it has to be wing mounted, and the wing has been set low in order to maintain the necessary ground clearance for the underfuselage stores. With a high-set wing, the main gear would have been too long, causing both retraction and stability problems. The YA-9 in fact could not carry underfuselage stores for just this reason. The A-10 has a total of 11 hardpoints, although a maximum of 10 can be used at one time. A trade-off was involved in this decision — ie underfuselage load-carrying ability against ease of maintenance — because almost all maintenance and repair work needs mobile platforms for access.

With the operational accent on low speed

Left:
The wing trailing edge virtually dismantles itself for
landing, as the decelerons and flaps deploy. Here a
weatherworn 57th FWW machine lands back at Nellis in
1980, carrying four Mavericks.   *Frank Mormillo*

Below left:
The subtle curves of the Hoerner wingtips, adopted both

to reduce drag and improve control, can be seen from two
different angles here.   *Fairchild*

Below:
The final assembly line is where the wings are mated to the
fuselage, the tail is nailed on, and the engine pods are
fitted. This picture probably shows the vast aileron, or
deceleron, area better than any other.   *Fairchild*

Below:
General Electric's TF34-GE-100 is a compact, high bypass ratio, non-augmented turbofan. The bypass ratio is determined by the relative size of the compressor, which can be seen to have a large diameter. *General Electric*

manoeuvrability, high lifting capacity and short-field performance, the main driving factors in the design were the wing and the power plants.

With a maximum speed requirement of just 400kt in level flight, a high aspect ratio wing with a large thickness/chord ratio was optimum to attain a high coefficient of lift. It was of course always possible that this speed would be exceeded in a dive, and the design team therefore settled on an airframe limiting speed of 450kt, Mach 0.68 under ICAO conditions. This allowed a highly cambered aerofoil section to be used, the NACA 6716 on the inboard section and the NACA 6713 outboard, with a thickness/chord ratio of 16%, more than three times thicker than the average fast jet. This comparatively deep section allowed a long and strong wing to be constructed for a fairly light weight. The centre section was constructed in a single piece notched into the underside of the fuselage, with bolted attachment points on the front and rear spars. The outer sections were canted up at a 7° dihedral angle, with downturned Hoerner-style tips, which reduce induced drag and tip vortices, improving both very low speed handling and cruise performance, the latter stated to be as much as 6-8%. The trailing-edge features a two-section single-slotted Fowler flap on each side, both for short field performance and for low speed manoeuvre, while well outboard are large tabbed ailerons. These are interesting in that they are split and can double as air brakes, with half opening upwards and the other half downwards. The main

gear retracts forwards into a housing projecting below the wing and forward of the leading edge, and between the housing and the fuselage is a leading-edge slat. Fuel tanks are located in the inboard wing section on either side of the fuselage.

At the time of the gestation period of the A-X, there were few serious contenders to power the new attack fighter. The survivability requirements demanded two engines, and this effectively eliminated anything propeller-driven, either reciprocating or turboprop. The diameter of a propeller would have dictated that the engines be set well out on the wings, with the attendant problems of asymmetric handling with one engine out. It would of course have been possible to couple them to a single propeller on the centreline, but this would have rendered the aircraft vulnerable to a single hit on the gearing. The orthodox turbojet had plenty of power for the job, but it was inefficient at the proposed operating speeds of the A-X, and the required endurance and radius of action would have involved using an unacceptably high fuel fraction, with all the weight, structure and protection problems inherent in this solution. There were, however, two high bypass ratio turbofans which were suitable, General Electric's TF34 and Lycoming's F-102. Of these the TF34 was further along the development path, and had more thrust than its rival. Moreover it had already been ordered into service as the engine for the new USN submarine hunter, the Lockheed S-3 Viking. A simple twin spool design, it promised considerable development potential. By contrast the Lycoming F-102 was less developed, less powerful and more complex, with the fan drive passing through the gearbox. Nevertheless, both A-X contenders had to submit proposals using both engines. In the event the YA-9 was powered by the F-102, while the YA-10 flew using the TF34.

There were several reasons why Fairchild Republic settled for the GE engine. It was more mature, simpler and easier to maintain, while the

Above:
The podded engine installation of the A-10A lends itself to ease of access, as this picture of it opened up shows. The upward cant of the nozzle is very evident. *Fairchild*

Left:
The TF34 is a modular engine, which greatly assists in reducing the time spent on repairs, as well as costs.
General Electric

Below:
A Boeing B-47 jet bomber was used as a test-bed for the initial trials of the TF34, which was mounted beneath the port wing. The TF34 has greater diameter but less length than the J47 turbojets, and is much more powerful and economical. *General Electric*

19

Above:
Shielding of the hot engine effluxes from ground-launched IR missiles is clearly shown here. Note the mottled Joint Attack Weapons System camouflage on two of the aircraft. *Frank Mormillo*

Left:
A close-up of the nose, showing the gun offset to port with the firing barrel on the centreline, the nose gear offset to starboard, and the ALR-46 RWR aerial housing. *Fairchild*

Right:
The forward retracting gear can be seen here as an A-10A of the 57th FWW takes off from Nellis. *Frank Mormillo*

additional power allowed a trade-off to be made in the airframe, of drag against cost, in the form of ease of construction and, with it, repairability. On the other hand the TF34 was heavier than its rival, and considerably more expensive, which was a serious consideration in a competition where cost was an important factor. As a result, GE modified the TF34 for A-X use, resulting in the TF34-GE-100. The two YA-10s used the Navy engine, but the -100 was installed in all others. Some titanium parts were replaced with steel, less attention was given to weight-saving processes, and certain specifically Navy kit was left off altogether. The result was an engine that was a bit cruder, a bit heavier, but cheaper and very reliable.

The most startling thing about the engines was their location, high mounted in pods towards the rear of the fuselage, in what at the time was called 'Caravelle' style, after the trend-setting French airliner. This position was chosen primarily with survivability in mind: while they were sufficiently close together so as not to pose a significant asymmetric handling problem with one engine out, they were sufficiently far apart to eliminate the possibility of both engines being taken out by a single hit, except by the very largest missiles. Nor could fuel from a ruptured tank spill into the combustor section, a form of battle damage guaranteed to cause an uncontrollable fire. The location also provided a measure of protection from heat-seeking surface-to-air missiles, a degree of shrouding being provided by the vertical and horizontal tail surfaces. The engine cowls were almost full length, and the bypass air from the fan would help to lower the IR signature of the exhaust plume. The final unconventional feature of the engines was that they were angled up at 9°. This would reduce the trim changes that always accompany changes in power settings, as well as giving an optimum thrust line on take-off. The high position also reduced the possibility of FOD ingestion on semi-prepared strips.

The high location was also a trade-off, as it made the engines difficult to get at for maintenance. This was however partially offset by ease of access, as the cowls were hinged at the top, exposing almost the entire engine. On the S-3 the TF34 had been mounted in underwing pods, and the engine bearers were situated at the top. This arrangement was continued on the -100, with cantilever mountings rather like ships' davits coming out of the fuselage. Hoisting provision was also incorporated, thus eliminating special lifting gear for an engine change. One unusual advantage of this particular location is that it permits service items to be done with the engines running.

The fuselage lines are extraordinarily simple, with straight lines and single curvatures except for the nose, where double curvatures could hardly be avoided. The muzzles of the gigantic GAU-8 cannon project from the underside of the nose, and are offset slightly to port, just enough so that the barrel that is firing is on the centreline at the critical moment, a very necessary precaution considering the enormous recoil forces involved. This has forced the nose gear, with its two landing lights, off to starboard a considerable distance, giving the A-10 a rather odd look from head-on. Like the main gear legs, the nose gear retracts forward. On top of the nose, and directly in front of the windscreen, is the in-flight refuelling receptacle.

The armoured cockpit is set well forward, 'near the crash' as one pilot observed, just above the breech mechanism of the gun and ahead of the huge magazine. The pilot sits up high on his

zero/zero ejection seat, with a forward view of 20° down over the nose, and 40° down over the sides. Good downward vision is essential for the CAS mission. The windshield consists of an optically flat bulletproof windscreen with curved quarterlights, the whole assembly hinging forward to permit access behind the instrument panel. The single-piece bubble canopy is hinged at the rear, and gives 360° vision above the plane of the aircraft, which is excellent for spotting air threats or looking back to observe the results of an attack, although it is restricted a bit by the large diameter turbofans. Access is from the left, via a rather flimsy-looking telescopic ladder housed beneath the instrument console.

From the cockpit backwards, the fuselage has an almost square section with a straight line taper to the rear. The 'black boxes' are located in a compartment over the gun ammunition magazine, and astern of this, fuel tanks extend back to a point just rearward of the engine intakes. Further back are the hydraulic reservoir and pumps, the air-conditioning system and other gear, and, very important, the auxiliary power unit (APU) which provides power for checking out the systems without the engines running and without the need for an external power source. It also enables the A-10 to self-start without the aid of ground support equipment. This is very important for an aircraft intended to operate from austere forward bases, as it reduces the amount of ground support needed.

Remarkably for a modern combat aircraft, the rear fuselage is almost empty, and carries little more than the control lines for the moving tail surfaces. The horizontal tail is of conventional, not to say old-fashioned, design, with a fixed plane and elevators, and easily detachable twin fins and rudders mounted on the extremes. The bottom of the fins is reinforced to act as a skid in the event of a wheels-up landing.

The avionics fit can only be described as basic. This was part of the austere philosophy intended to keep costs down. Both VHF and UHF communications kit was fitted, and a TV display for the electro-optical Maverick was located in the top right-hand corner of the instrument panel. A Kaiser Head Up Display (HUD) was fitted, and an ALR-46 Radar Warning Receiver (RWR). Navigation was originally to be carried out using Tacan

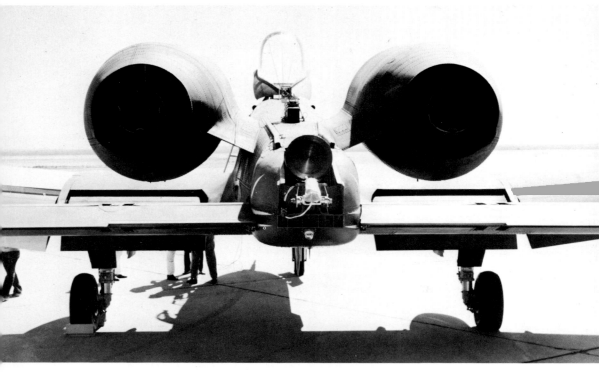

beacons, and the altimeter was of the atmospheric pressure type. In practice much of this was found to be inadequate and either upgraded or replaced.

This then was pretty much the intended aircraft when the first YA-10 took to the air from Edwards AFB on 10 May 1972, with Fairchild Chief Test Pilot Sam Nelson at the controls. It was followed on the 30th of that month by the first YA-9, which meant that both first flights were ahead of schedule. The second prototypes of each first flew on 21 July and 23 August respectively. The time before the official fly-off was spent in examining the flight envelope for potential problems, as once the evaluation had begun, no changes could be made unless flight safety was at risk. The only serious problem found involved the YA-10, and was due to the unorthodox engine location. At high angles of attack, distorted airflow from the forebody entered the intakes, and could cause engine compressor stalling. This was countered for the evaluation by an automatic system that reduced power just before the stall. At a later date a permanent fix was introduced; a short vertical fence was placed on each side of the fuselage just ahead of the wing leading-edge, the leading-edge slats (previously described) were added to the wing centre section, short stall strips were fixed to the leading-edge outboard of the main gear housing, and finally a fillet was fitted at the junction of the wing trailing-edge and the fuselage. At this point

Left:
The second YA-10 was fitted with this spin chute compartment at the rear of the fuselage for spin trials. It was found to be hard to make it spin, and easy to recover. *USAF*

Below:
The frame of the Kaiser Electronics HUD can be clearly seen, as can the node aerials of the RWR on the nose. *USAF*

Above:
Early bombing trials, and the first YA-10 hauls a heavy load of Mk 82 slicks out to the range. *Fairchild*

the GAU-8 was not ready and all the evaluation aircraft carried the six-barrel M61 20mm cannon. Appearances apart, the main difference between the Fairchild and the Northrop contenders was that the YA-10 was close to being a production machine, whereas the YA-9 was more the traditional prototype.

The Air Force A-X flight evaluation began on 10 October 1972, and lasted to 9 December. The flying was carried out by five pilots who formed the A-X Joint Test Force: three test pilots from Air Force Systems Command (AFSC) — Col Buzz Lynch, the JTF Director, Maj Larry Fortner and Capt Roy Bridges — and two pilots from Tactical Air Command (TAC) — Maj Dick Clark and Capt Al Barnes. During the preceding July and August, the JTF pilots had flown 10 sorties each in the A-37, practising the attack profiles that would be flown in the evaluation.

Over the next 60 days, 180 sorties were flown, for a total flight time of 284 hours, of which two-fifths was spent in measuring the accuracy of weapons delivery. Pilot quality variation was ruled out by the simple expedient of swapping aircraft — flying the YA-10 today meant flying the YA-9 tomorrow — while the attack profiles were constantly varied in terms of heading and dive angle, so that pilot proficiency in one particular form of attack could not influence the results. Nor could wind or weather make any difference; the aircraft flew in pairs, and if one could not go, the other did not.

Visual targets were built at Dagrag Range, and more than 600 practice bombs were delivered from each type. Bombing attacks were made at three different dive angles, 20°, 45° and 60°, with a heading change after each pass. Strafing passes from both low and high angles were also made on each range mission, and a total of 556 targets were riddled. Data was gathered from radar, telemetry and closed circuit television during the attacks.

Other trials included operational suitability missions, which were flown by the two TAC pilots.

25

Below:
This was the first YA-10 to be fitted with the GAU-8/A. This view also shows the degree to which the nose gear is offset to port, while slats have been added to the inboard leading-edge sections. The black protuberance ahead of the nose gear leg houses antennae for the ALR-46 RWR. *Fairchild*

Inset:
Carrying tandem triplets of bombs on the inboard stations, the first YA-10 is displayed to the public for the first time at Edwards AFB in May 1972. *Frank Mormillo*

These were the only times when the competing aircraft were not in the air together, as they involved formation tactics. Three differing missions were flown, a total of 12 sorties, with the two TAC pilots alternating as leader and wingman. One involved armed escort for helicopters, the second was an armed reconnaissance, and the third was defensive air combat against the Phantoms of nearby George AFB. Capt Barnes later recalled 'we asked both airplanes to do everything they may ever have to do. Both of them handle real well. In fact, I'm amazed at how well they manoeuvre. They can roll with any fighter'. In fact the YA-9 handled rather better than the YA-10, mainly due to a lower inertia moment in the lateral plane attributable to its more orthodox engine layout.

On the ground, the manufacturers were responsible for maintenance, carefully observed by a team of 26 technicians from the JTF who monitored maintenance times, special tools required, skill levels, accessibility and even the number of fasteners to be opened. Here the YA-10 was ahead, although not by a significant amount.

At the end of the day there was little to choose between them; the range results for both were good. The YA-9 had a unique direct side force control system, pitting airbrakes against rudder to allow the aircraft to 'sidestep' in the attack run without changing bank angle, which should have made it easier to line up on target for greater accuracy; but differences seem to have been marginal.

The only two items not evaluated in the fly-off were the gun, which was still not available, and survivability. Here Air Force Systems Command entered the picture. All the YA-9's fuel was carried in the wings, as was a fair amount of the fuel of the YA-10. Mock-ups of the wings complete with tanks were mounted in a wind tunnel and shot at using a Soviet-made 23mm cannon. Some 33 different wing configurations were used for the YA-9, and 26 for the YA-10. The fuselage tanks in the YA-10 were also tested, no less than 35 configurations being tried. Other AFSC trials tested the respective merits of

aluminium, ceramic and titanium armour. Out of this came the titanium 'bathtub' surrounding the cockpit of the A-10. The evaluation aircraft were without this feature, although the missing weight was more than offset by the more than 2,000lb of instrumentation carried by each.

Analysis of the evaluation was complete by early January 1973, and on the 18th of that month it was announced that the Fairchild aircraft was the winner. There was never much in it, but the greater survivability of the unorthodox layout of the YA-10 tipped the scales. This announcement was followed on 1 March by a cost-plus incentive fee contract to continue testing and build 10 (later reduced to six) pre-production aircraft. At the same time, General Electric was awarded a development contract for 32 TF34 engines to power them. Meanwhile gun development was making progress, and on 14 June, General Electric of Burlington was selected to develop the GAU-8 system.

The reduction of the proposed 10 pre-production aircraft to six came about as the result of political pressure. The United States Congress was not convinced that the A-10 could do anything better than the A-7D Corsair II already in service, and insisted on a formal evaluation. As we all know to our cost, politicians are instant experts on any subject, including defence matters, and they were unable to understand the concept of a slow mover jet. The USAF carried out paper evalu-ations of the A-10 against the A-4 Skyhawk, the A-7D Corsair, and a proposed modified Corsair, the A-7DER, which was to carry the GAU-8 cannon. Actually this A-7 variant involved a major rebuild, with a longer fuselage, a more powerful engine and other modifications which would have made it an expensive option. It could not have carried anywhere near the same amount of gun ammunition as the A-10, and its survivability would have been much less. The Air Force evaluation, called Saber Armor Charlie, came down firmly in favour of the A-10, but the politicians, backed by the Army, still called for a fly-off.

Meanwhile, the Air Force showed precisely what it thought of the A-10 by devoting the entire summer edition of the Tactical Air Warfare Center Review to a feature on the aircraft by Maj Michael J. Major, of the Fighter/Attack Directorate. After a reasoned discussion of the A-10 and its role, he concluded with a light-hearted comment which was to affect the A-10 ever after.

'One last thought in closing — Fairchild-Republic's last several aircraft have been affectionately nicknamed "hogs". The F-84s were "hogs" (straight-wing) and "super hogs" (swept-wing). The F-105, most commonly known as the "Thud", was also referred to as the "ultra-hog". What do you suppose the A-10 will be called — the "wart-hog"?' The name stuck, despite the later official christening of Thunderbolt II, following the 1940s vintage Republic fighter, the P-47 Thunderbolt.

The flight test programme continued throughout 1973 and 1974 using the two YA-10s, albeit at a reduced rate. The second machine was used for static proof load testing before being returned to flight test status in October 1973 with certain aerodynamic refinements, aimed at reducing drag. The cockpit enclosure was smoothed a little, the engine nacelles reduced in length and made sleeker, while the landing gear housings were reduced in cross-section. Most importantly, the wing span was increased by some 2.5ft, while the slats described earlier were made retractable. These improvements were all featured in the production aircraft. The first GAU-8 was installed in the original prototype in November 1973, and flight testing commenced in February 1974.

With Congressional pressure mounting, the flight evaluation against the A-7D could not be long delayed. One of the chief difficulties was formulating a test programme that would be fair to

both types. The A-X fly-off techniques could not be used due to disparity of performance. If the A-10 was tied to the wing of the A-7, the trial would end one minute after take-off as the A-7 dwindled into the distance, while in the opposite case, either the A-7 would be spat out the first time the A-10 turned, or it would quickly hit bingo fuel and have to break off and seek a tanker. The trials were flown at Fort Riley in Kansas between 16 April and 10 May 1974, with four participating pilots flying both aircraft in turn. The flights were centred around the CAS mission, and they succeeded in confirming what the USAF had been saying all along; that a slow mover was far more suitable for the task. The last obstacle had now been removed, and on 31 July 1974 the Department of Defense gave initial authorisation for the production of 52 aircraft.

Late in 1974, initial gun firing trials had shown up a potential problem. It should be remembered that both the gun and the ammunition were also in the development phase at this time. The propellant was not being completely burned before the projectile left the barrel, but was igniting shortly after, in the form of a large fireball. The cure was simple; the burn speed was increased by adding a small amount of potassium nitrate to the charge. With all the propellant burning inside the barrel, the muzzle velocity was improved for good measure.

The tempo increased in 1975. On 15 February the first pre-production A-10A made its first flight from Edwards AFB, just one day after the two YA-10s had logged 1,000 hours flight time. This machine, No 73-1664, conducted performance and handling quality tests, flutter and air load

demonstrations up to 100% of the limiting load. It was not fitted with the GAU-8, but carried a great deal of instrumentation. The second, 73-1665, made its first flight from the old company airfield at Farmingdale on 26 April, to commence armament tests, stores certification and weapons sub-system evaluations. It was joined on 10 June by 73-1666, slated to carry out sub-system evaluations and weapons delivery accuracy. This was followed at monthly intervals by the final three pre-production machines, assigned to performance and propulsion evaluation; initial operational test and evaluation; and climatic tests respectively. As new aircraft joined the team, the two YA-10s were retired, having logged a total of 821 flights and 1,139.4 flying hours. Then, on 21 October, the first production A-10A, s/n 75-00258, made its first flight from Farmingdale.

The first live firing against armoured targets by a GAU-8-equipped A-10A came on 13 November, on the Nellis ranges. A total of 15 main battle tanks, including American M48s and Russian T-62s obtained via Israel, were subjected to a gun attack. The lower rate of fire, 2,100 rounds per minute, was selected to increase the persistence during the trial, and the loading was five armour piercing to each high explosive incendiary. A single A-10A made 24 passes at the tanks from the

Left:
Only the two YA-10s carried the full USAF markings as shown here. The basic finish is pale gloss grey, with red stripes on engine nacelles and black 'no walk' lines on the wings. *Fairchild*

Below:
This Maverick-equipped early production aircraft displays its wingtip mounted airbrakes as it comes in to touch down on the dry bed of Bicycle Lake. *Fairchild*

eft:

**he second pre-production aircraft on carry trials with
nart weapons; on the left a TV-guided GBU-8; on the
ght a GBU-10 laser-guided weapon.** *Fairchild*

elow:

**Inly the YA-10 prototypes and pre-production A-10As
arried nose probes, which occupied the flight refuelling
eceptacle area. Close scrutiny reveals what appears to be
ordite strips set in the canopy, a feature not shared by
roduction models.** *Fairchild*

ottom:

**he second YA-10 taxies out for a test flight in September
977. The port wing and fin were painted white for high
sibility during spin testing.** *Frank Mormillo*

rear, firing one- or two-second bursts from an
average range of 3,000ft. The results convinced the
doubters; seven tanks were completely destroyed
and the remaining eight put out of action, either
immobilised or with jammed turrets.

Further testing and evaluation continued for
some considerable time, but there was by now no
doubt that the A-10A was a winner. AGM-65
Maverick was successfully cleared for use, giving
the tank-buster a stand-off capability, while the
fourth production aircraft, 75-00261, was delivered
to TACs 355th TTW at Davis-Monthan AFB in
Arizona on its first flight on 14 February 1976. The
first combat wing to receive the type, the 354th
TFW based at Myrtle Beach, South Carolina, took
delivery of its first Warthog in March 1977, and the
first squadron in the wing to become operational,
the 356th TFS, did so the following October.

3 Survivability, Repairability, Maintainability

It is an inescapable fact that in wartime, aircraft will be shot down and their pilots lost. An aircraft taking a direct hit from a large missile will inevitably go down, but direct hits from large missiles are the exception rather than the rule. Historically, aircraft have far more often been lost to smaller weapons fortuitously hitting them in a vulnerable spot, or to damage sustained from a proximity burst of a large weapon. Peter Borgaert, writing in *International Defense Review* in 1977, categorised kills into four classes: those that occurred within two seconds of being hit, those that occurred within 15 seconds, followed by 5min and 15min kills. The first two categories imply that catastrophic damage was inflicted — structural failure, explosion, uncontrollable fire or incapacitation of the pilot. With the exception of explosion, the inference is that the 15sec kills were caused by damage of less severity than those of the 2sec kills. The 5min kills could also be the result of fire, aerodynamic forces acting on a damaged structure, or loss of hydraulic power leading to ultimate loss of control, while 15min (or even longer) kills could be due to such things as hits on the undercarriage (causing the aircraft to b written off on landing) or possibly a fuel lea making it impossible for the aircraft to reach friendly field. The interesting part of the articl was the frequency of such kills; for each 2sec ki there were three 15sec kills, eight 5min kills and n less than 15 15min kills. The obvious inference that the majority of aircraft lost in combat fa victim of less than catastrophic damage, at th ratio of nearly 6:1. There is obviously a lot of scop for making aircraft less vulnerable.

Analysis of combat losses in both the Vietnan and Middle East wars gave the following result Fire was the main enemy, with hits on the fue system accounting for no less than 62% of losse followed by pilot incapacitation 18%, flyin controls 10%, loss of engine power 7%, an structural damage just 3%. If the vulnerability the fuel system and the pilot could be halved, som 40% of the overall losses could be eliminated although this would of course have the effect increasing the percentages in other areas: flyin controls would go up to 17%, engine power t 12% and structural damage to 5%.

SYSTEM COMPONENT	HISTORIC FREQUENCY OF LOSSES COMBAT LOSS %			WEIGHT OF A-10A SURVIVAL PROVISIONS – KILOGRAMS
	20	40	60	
Fuel System				513
Pilot				666
Flight Controls				73
Single Engine				–
Structure and Misc				57
Dual Engines				–
Ammunition Drum	Not available but minimal			132

Combat Losses
Historic causes of combat losses used to design A-10A survivability provisions.

TOTAL	1441

A-10A Vulnerability to 23mm API/HEI

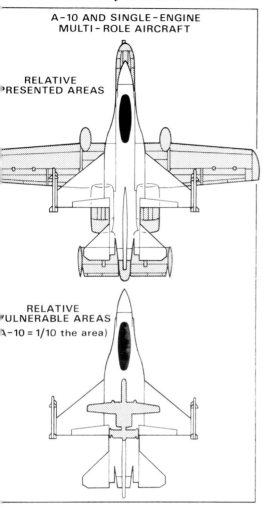

**A-10 AND SINGLE-ENGINE
MULTI-ROLE AIRCRAFT**

RELATIVE
PRESENTED AREAS

RELATIVE
VULNERABLE AREAS
(A-10 = 1/10 the area)

Above:

Despite its comparatively large presented area, the A-10 is only one-tenth as vulnerable to 23mm AA fire as a typical single-engine multi-role aircraft.

The time-honoured way of improving an aircraft's survivability in the ground attack mission has been to make it faster, with a modicum of armour for protection. The mission demands that the aircraft expose itself to the defences, and the idea was to make it a more difficult target, while protecting it against a lucky hit, although total invulnerability against ground fire has never been a practical proposition due to the weight of protection needed. Protection has always been a trade-off against performance and load-carrying ability. Much depends upon the strength of the defences. A direct hit by a large projectile will nearly always be lethal, but large weapons are in the minority, due to a combination of expense and mobility, while smaller weapons are often not so effective, and need a multiplicity of hits to accumulate enough damage to be fatal. In this connection it should be noted that in the October War of 1973, Israeli Skyhawks suffered no less than 26 hits from shoulder-launched SA-7 heat-seeking missiles, but all except two recovered safely to base with varying degrees of damage which took them out of the war until repairs could be effected. On the other hand, while MiGs and SAMs posed a serious threat in South-East Asia, the majority of American losses were caused by gunfire, often of the light and medium calibre radar-laid type.

From this it could be seen that much could be done to make an aircraft survivable, especially when, as in the case of the A-10A, high performance could be traded for weight of protection. The first measure for survivability was to avoid being hit, and speed was the traditional way of achieving this, as it greatly reduced the time that the aircraft was within range of the defences. The fast movers in Vietnam approached the target at medium altitude, above the effective range of the guns, and attacked in a dive, pulling up and out at high speed. This method was usable under the circumstances, but contained disadvantages in other scenarios. Clear visibility was needed for visual weapons aiming, and this worked two ways, as the ground gunners had plenty of time to see the attack coming and prepare to meet it. A high speed attack meant a long slant range, which reduced accuracy. Finally, against a strong, multi-layered defensive system, it would have been extremely dangerous.

The A-10A had been deliberately designed to deliver weapons accurately, and speed was a trade-off to this end. However, its low speed manoeuvrability could be used to conceal its approach by hiding down in the weeds behind hills, the treeline, or even buildings. In VFR (visual flight rules) conditions, the limiting factor in low level flight is the pilot's ability to avoid impacting the ground, and in this regime the A-10A is excellent. Operational altitude is frequently determined by the capability of the defences, but the ground always rates 100%.

The first survivability attribute of the A-10A is therefore its ability to make a stealthy approach, using terrain masking, followed by a quick break from cover, aim and fire, and a rapid turning dive back into shelter, which reduces the time that it is at hazard. Stealthy approach or no, the A-10A can hardly be described as a stealth aircraft. It is too large and too angular, and has a radar cross-section to match, while the visual signature aids easy recognition at a distance. On the other hand, it will try to stay out of sight as much as possible, which equally means out of the line of sight of enemy radars. A byproduct of its large size and ungainly profile is that it is hardly likely to be misidentified, and attacked by 'friendly' forces. By contrast, its IR signature is low and it is a quiet machine, only about half as noisy as an F-4 Phantom in military power — although as the

Right:
Although a 7.62mm armour-piercing bullet made a bit of a mess of the A-10A windshield on trials, it was not penetrated, nor was there any interior spalling. *Fairchild*

Below:
The titanium bathtub protecting the cockpit was subjected to stringent tests. Four 23mm and one 37mm HEI shells were fired at this panel at point-blank range without once penetrating. *Fairchild*

Below right:
The reverse view of the same panel, showing the absence of spalling. A similar hit in this area of any other aircraft would incapacitate the pilot, to say the least. *Fairchild*

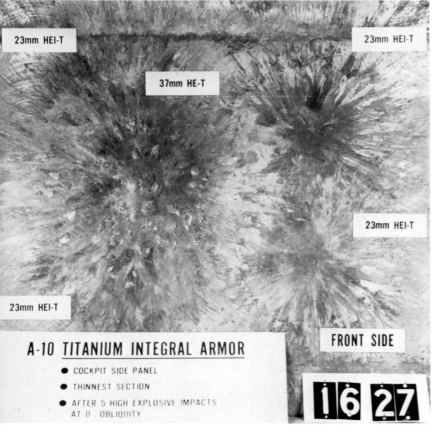

23mm HEI-T

23mm HEI-T

37mm HE-T

23mm HEI-T

23mm HEI-T

A-10 TITANIUM INTEGRAL ARMOR
- COCKPIT SIDE PANEL
- THINNEST SECTION
- AFTER 5 HIGH EXPLOSIVE IMPACTS AT 0 OBLIQUITY

FRONT SIDE

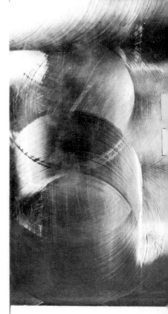

A-10 TITANIUM
- COCKPIT SIDE
- THINNEST SE
- AFTER 5 HIGH AT 0 OBLIQU

Above:
The cockpit of the pre-production A-10A used in the fly-off against the A-7 Corsair in 1974. *USAF*

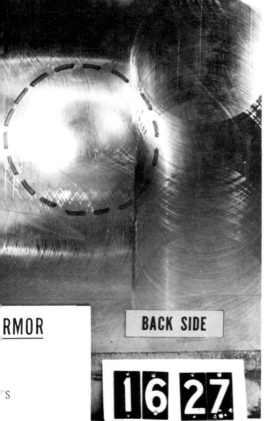

RMOR

BACK SIDE

16 27

battlefield is a noisy place, this is not much of a consideration.

The primary cause of aircraft losses in combat is fire; this is hardly surprising when one considers that the average fighter carries some three to four tons of the highly volatile liquid, plus hydraulic fluid which is also inflammable, and lubricant which is less so. One of the more common causes of uncontrollable fire is a ruptured tank spilling fuel into the engine. The high mounted outboard location of the engines virtually eliminates this possibility. The inboard wing sections carry integral tanks, and as these are the most vulnerable, the fuel in them is used first. The wing tanks are self-sealing and are filled with reticulated foam which inhibits leakage and the spread of fire, while greatly reducing the risk of an explosion. Tests carried out in a wind tunnel at Wright-Patterson AFB saw more than 250 23mm API and HEI shells fired at mock-ups of the A-10 fuel tanks from point-blank range, in a simulated slipstream of 400kt, together with many shells of other calibres, without causing a single explosion. The greater amount of internal fuel is carried in two large fuselage tanks, which, as they have a small presented area in relation to their capacity, are less vulnerable to hits. They are also self-sealing and filled with foam, while the voids around them are

also packed with foam so that in the event of
damage causing a serious fuel loss, the chance of
the slipstream vaporising the fuel into an explosive
fuel/air mix is minimised. Each tank has cut-off
valves, and the fuel lines are situated within the
tanks for extra protection. The fuel lines to the
engines are protected with a self-sealing sheath,
and are led up and over the top of the nacelles,
where they are best protected from ground fire.
Two sump tanks provide a 'get home' supply for
absolute emergencies. As the tanks are situated
closely around the aircraft's centre of gravity, no
fuel transfer system is necessary. The total weight
of protection to the fuel system amounts to some
1,080lb.

Protection for the pilot amounts to an even
greater weight, 1,357lb in total, even though

Above:
A mock-up of the cockpit was made and mounted on rails
to test the Escapac ejection seat. The Escapac has since
been supplanted by the ACES II seat. *Fairchild*

Right:
This sequence of three pictures shows an early test of the
ejection seat using a dummy pilot (no rude remarks
please) from a rocket-propelled sled at Holloman AFB,
New Mexico. *Fairchild*

compromises had to be made to give him an adequate view out and down. The windshield is bulletproof, and the canopy is of heavyweight material well able to stop shell fragments. The pilot is seated in a titanium 'bathtub' which gives protection against direct hits from 23mm API shells. Various materials were evaluated before titanium was chosen, including ceramics and aluminium. During trials no less than 430 rounds of 23mm were fired at the cockpit bath, the sides of which vary between ½in and 1½in thick, the variation depending on what other structure lies between the armour and the skin, and also the most likely angles of strike; 37mm rounds of HE were also fired and failed to penetrate. The kinetic energy of such an impact is very great, and the risk, apart from penetration, is that of spalling, in which the impact knocks flakes of metal off the inside of the armour, which would then travel around inside the cockpit at high velocity. To negate the effects of spalling, the bathtub is lined with a multiple layer of nylon. The bathtub is the heaviest single item of armour on the A-10A, weighing 1,200lb.

The flying controls are the next greatest area of potential loss. Like most of its contemporaries, the A-10A has a dual hydraulic control system, although this is widely spaced to prevent a single hit taking both circuits out, each circuit running in a protected duct. Unlike them, it has a manual back-up, with a duplicated cable system. If one system jams it can be cut off and the other used. The A-10A can also survive the loss of many of its flight control surfaces; an elevator, rudder, or deceleron missing might mean an early return to base but it does not mean the loss of the aircraft. Alternative flight control modes are also available in extreme circumstances. Trim tabs are available on both ailerons and elevators, while pitch control can be achieved by using the air brakes, partial roll by using the rudders, while differential thrust from the widely spaced engines can produce yaw. As the landing gear is operated by a hydraulic system, perhaps it ought to be considered here.

The main gear is of very simple design, and retracts forward, as does the nose gear. If the hydraulics are out, unlocking the gear will allow it to descend under the influence of gravity, locking automatically when the maximum point of travel is reached, to permit a safe, conventional landing. When retracted, the main wheels are still partly exposed, and if the gear jams in the up position,

Right:
With such a strong accent on systems redundancy, it is rather surprising that the landing gear has only single wheels. Nevertheless, both nose and main gears retract forward, and in the event of hydraulic failure, whatever the reason, the gears can drop by gravity, locking into place through the force of the airflow. *Fairchild*

Below:
The enormous GAU-8/A gun and its huge ammunition drum fit snugly into the space provided with little room to spare. *Fairchild*

project sufficiently beneath the aircraft to protect the underside from significant damage in the event of a wheels-up landing. The unusual main gear fairing beneath the wing was adopted to eliminate any break in the wing structural members, which would have caused a weak point.

The gun ammunition is another vulnerable point in any fighter, but more so in the A-10A because of the large amount of propellant in the 30mm shells, and their very large number. There is a tremendous difference in size between a magazine holding 500 20mm shells as in the F-16, and 1,350 of the large 30mm shells as in the Warthog, and the simple fact is that as it is bigger, it is more likely to be hit, and if it were to be penetrated, the resulting explosion would be far more severe. The ammunition drum of the A-10A is set as far from the aircraft skin as possible, and is not only armoured but is surrounded by aluminium trigger plates of varying thicknesses designed to detonate an HE round before hitting the armour.

The main form of protection against aircraft loss through lack of power is the fact that it has two engines, and that these are too widely spaced to be taken out by a single hit except of the most massive kind. In fact it is stated that an engine pod can be shot clean off without involving the loss of the aircraft. The fans have an armour belt around them, but this is essential in any case to contain the blades in the event of a catastrophic failure. The solid titanium blades, turning at a sedate rate by jet standards, have proved remarkably resistant to both bird strike, an ever-present threat at low

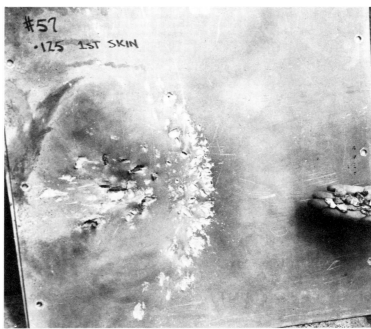

#57
.125 1ST SKIN

Above:
The ammunition drum is protected by spaced armour. Shown here is the effect of a 23mm HEI shell, the fragments of which are being held to the right of the picture. *Fairchild*

Left:
The finishing touch is added to the fin of the fifth pre-production aircraft. The fins and rudders are interchangeable and redundant; one side can be shot clean off and the aircraft will still recover to base. The rather obvious riveting is a feature of the Warthog, whose low speed does not demand a clean finish. *Fairchild*

level, and FOD. The high setting is an excellent anti-FOD measure. The high bypass turbofans give a small IR footprint, which is further masked against ground-launched heat-seeking missiles by the position of the horizontal and vertical tail surfaces. The one vulnerable aspect of the engines comes in the event of a double flame-out. The relight speed of the TF34 is rather higher than the maximum speed of a clean A-10A in level flight. To achieve relight speed, the aircraft must be dived, and the average operational height just does not permit this. This has led to a standing joke among fast jet drivers that the Warthog is the only aircraft in service that is faster with its engines out than with them at full throttle. This was capped by a Warthog driver who commented that the A-10A was the only aircraft he knew that got bird strikes from behind!

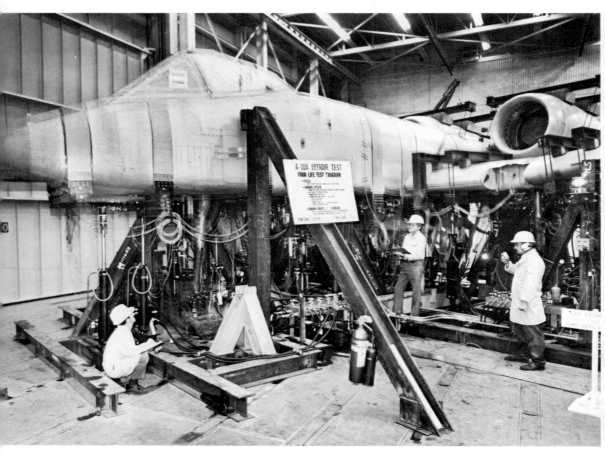

Structural damage as a cause of loss came out at a low percentage in the USAF analysis of losses in Vietnam and the Middle East, but with all the preventative measures taken to increase survivability in other areas, it began to assume an increasing importance. The g limitation of the A-10A was set at 7.33 at the design stage, which combined with a safety factor of 1.5, gave an ultimate limit of 11g, at a nominal combat weight of 30,000lb, falling to 5g and 7.5g at maximum all-up weight.

Apart from systems duplication, the A-10A was built to be tough, using redundant load paths throughout the structure. The vertical and horizontal tail surfaces are three-sparred, as are the wings, which are fixed to the fuselage with four bolted attachment points. The aircraft can survive the loss of one wing attachment or one spar being completely severed, or two opposing longerons in the fuselage being cut. It can continue to fly with an engine nacelle missing, a complete horizontal and vertical tail surface missing from one side, or an outboard wing section shot off, and survive the loss of all the control surfaces on one wing, plus great lumps of surface missing.

This survival capability has been regarded by some commentators as an admission that the A-10A is going to get hit, and that the fast jet, avoiding the defences with sheer speed, is actually less vulnerable. This totally overlooks the mission concept, which is to stay in the battle area for extended periods, making multiple attacks with great accuracy. The fast jet is essentially a single-pass attacker lacking the accuracy of the A-10A; if it returns to make multiple passes, it too is going to get hit; and, without the survivability of the Fairchild aircraft, is going to be shot down if the defences are any good at all.

Repairability and maintainability are the other two strong points of the A-10A. Some three-quarters of the surface area most at risk is designed to be repaired, by a 'band-aid' patch if the damage is slight, or replaced in the field. The fins and rudders, engines, slats, inboard flaps and the main gear units are designed to be non-handed, and are interchangeable from one side to the other. If an A-10A gets really badly shot about, the field repairs are likely to take too long, it becomes a 'hangar queen', to be cannibalised for spares.

Left:
The photographer's hand wasn't shaking: the aircraft was. The fatigue and stress article is seen being tested to the equivalent of four lifetimes. *Fairchild*

Right:
Crew Chief Art Burgess climbs the ladder to confer with pilot Lt Mark Riley after a mission. His name is stencilled on the aircraft beneath that of the pilot. *Frank Mormillo*

Below:
The windshield hinges forward to allow access behind the instrument panel, while other hatches open to reveal the avionics compartments. *Frank Mormillo*

Survivability not only gets the pilot back safely, it also brings back a supply of much needed spares.

The A-10A is not only designed to be repairable, it is also designed for ease of maintenance. An aircraft on the ground for essential maintenance is an aircraft not available for operations. The original target set for maintenance man-hours per flight hour was 12; during the initial flight test and fly-off phase, Fairchild nearly halved this time, and the A-10A has since achieved an enviable reputation for serviceability. In an operational unit, each aircraft has a crew chief assigned to it, who supervises and assists on all maintenance and repairs jobs. Sgt John Bylack, from Chicago, is a man built on the same lines as the aircraft in his charge, large and solid. He has been an A-10A crew chief for three years, and in late 1986 was responsible for aircraft No 160 of the 81st TFW based at RAF Bentwaters.

'A lot of people say that the job is easy, because we do a lot of launch and recovery; that's part of our job, we park them and then have to fuel them. That's easy enough, but it gets pretty intense when you have so many aircraft flying. There is much more depth on the maintenance side, because you have a hand in every job on the flight line, except where weapons are concerned. That's because they have so many different weapons, all with their own safety rules, so we just let the weapons people come in and do their thing.

'The crew chief has his own private airplane, and he takes a great pride in it. When it returns from a mission, he helps recover it, and is the first person the pilot sees after landing. The pilot tells him the problems encountered on the mission, and he asks the questions that will enable him to understand the fault properly. The pilot usually talks a lot more to the crew chief than anyone else because he

Above:
Technicians top up the oxygen of this Connecticut ANG aircraft in wintry conditions. *Frank Mormillo*

Top right:
Warm air is used to overcome icing conditions, as demonstrated here by a 174th TFW, New York Air

National Guard, crew, during a deployment to Lechfeld in Germany in March 1981. *USAF*

Right:
An indication of the size of the Warthog is given in this view of a ground crewman clearing ice from the tail surfaces of a 103rd TFG aircraft. *Frank Mormillo*

Below:
**Loading the gun and discharging the empties would be a
mammoth task without the aid of the Hydra ALS
(ammunition loading system), seen here in action.
Forward basing is all very well, but one specialised piece
of kit the A-10A cannot do without is the ALS.**
Frank Mormillo

es him a lot more, and they build up a mutual
ust. I am supposed to inspect the jet after the last
ight of the day, and if anything is wrong, get it
xed. It has its own APU, so if we want to run it
p, we don't have to wait for support equipment to
rive. We check out the fuel, oxygen, and all the
ghting systems; we select the hydraulics and
neck out the flight controls. When the pilot
rives next morning, the jet is ready to fly. If we
p find any problems, the jet is broke out right
ere and we fix it.

'Each section of airplanes has its own specific
aintenance crews who are specialists in various
chnical fields, and I call whichever crew I need to
elp me. I have an assistant crew chief, and we are
cks of all trades, masters of none. Some of the
aintenance fields we can really help out though.
ay I've an engine problem. I break the engine
wls and have a look. Though I'm not an engine
pert, I am fairly familiar with it through the
aintenance schools I've attended, and can detect
ch things as an integrated drive leak or
hatever. When my engine person comes out, I
n help him change it, and get the plane back
gether to fly that afternoon, we've done it many
nes. The engine is real easy to get at.

'There are plenty of other maintenance fields for
e to help out, like the electronics, the air
nditioning, the windshield washer, and other
b-systems. Every crew chief is trained in
draulics and in other fields. If I have a hydraulic
oblem, I know whether to use a high or low
essure line. The Air Force demands a lot of
ing out of the A-10A, and it can take a lot of

hard usage, and you have to keep on top of the
maintenance, but if you have the right people, no
task takes more than two hours. Even changing a
major flight control, a rudder or a deceleron, can
be done in less than that.'

Questioned on battle damage, Sgt Bylack outlined
the procedures.

'Returning after battle damage, the airplane pulls
into the assessor's area. He estimates, after
assessing the area of damage, how long it will take
to fix, and what time it should be fixed. He writes
on the outside what is wrong: wiring, structural
damage, hydraulic damage or whatever. Then it is
taken into a hardened shelter where we've got a
battle damage repair kit which contains every tool
we need to repair the aircraft in the least amount
of time. Let's say that the torque box of the wing is
hit. The undercarriage hydraulic troop, the sheet
metal guys, and the crew chief are all in on it. The
crew chief is trained to tear the exterior portion of
the skin apart, look into the damage, and decide
what needs to be done, such as whether to take a
hydraulic line out or to cut it in half and splice it.
He is also responsible for reinforcing the structure,
fitting the right angle iron to a spar or rib, then
replacing the damaged section with the right skin,
even down to using the right rivets. The A-10 is
easy to repair because it's open spaced. Say you
get a damaged control cable running between two
spars; there is so much room that you have easy
access to swage a broken cable and allow it to pass
through the bulkhead or spar or whatever.'

Sgt Bylack confirms that the Warthog is easy to
work on, simple to both maintain and repair, and
that access is easy to virtually everything. Like
everyone else connected with the A-10A, he is a
fan.

4 The Weapons

If the A-10A is an unusual aircraft, then so is the gun that it was designed to carry. The gun armament unit (GAU) -8/A Avenger is the largest, heaviest, longest ranged and most destructive cannon ever carried by an aircraft. Before proceeding, perhaps we should define one or two points. The difference between a machine gun and a cannon lies in the calibre: anything below 15mm calibre is a machine gun while 15mm and upwards is a cannon. Machine guns fire bullets while cannon fire shells. This needs to be said because many sources refer to the GAU-8/A firing bullets, and it is normally referred to as a gun rather than a cannon, and confusion can sometimes arise.

The requirement to kill main battle tanks with a gun was, and still is, a difficult one, and is exacerbated when the gun has to be mounted in an aircraft. Modern tanks carry large guns of 105mm calibre or more with which to oppose their own kind, relying on single shots using a heavy projectile, launched from a stationary or relatively slow moving, very stable platform. Such a gun could not possibly be mounted in a tactical aircraft, and even if it could, the level of accuracy necessary to achieve a worthwhile proportion of single shot kills would be beyond the state of the art. The

question also arises, why was a gun chosen when smart anti-tank weapons were becoming available? The answer lies in the state of the art at the time when the A-X requirement was first mooted. A tank is a small target, and heavily armoured, and is relatively impervious to blast and fragments; only a direct hit will do. Neither laser nor electro optical guidance would give this type of accuracy; some direct hits would inevitably be scored, but not enough. Compared with an aircraft, a tank is a relatively cheap battlefield asset. In purely financial terms, an anti-tank aircraft has to knock out a given number of tanks to reach the break-even point, possibly as many as 15, before it itself is lost. Smart weapons aggravate the situation even more, as they themselves are expensive. The Vietnam experience demonstrated convincingly that not too much faith should be put into

Below:
A pilot's helmet gives scale to the massive seven-barrel rotor assembly of the GAU-8/A cannon. The shells have been described as 'milk bottle sized'. This is slightly misleading; while the height is about correct, they are much slimmer. *General Electric*

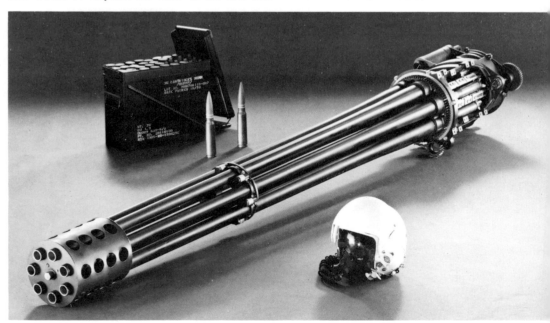

48

theoretical kill probabilities where guided missiles were concerned, and until such time as worthwhile figures could be achieved under realistic rather than laboratory range conditions, something simpler and more reliable was needed. Like a gun!

The anti-tank aircraft has one great advantage over the tank; it can work around its target and hit it from the sides, the rear and on top, where the armour is thinner, whereas tank guns have in most cases to penetrate the thick frontal armour. This eased the problem considerably, and a 30mm projectile calibre was selected as the best compromise between lethality and system weight and size, while the inherent inaccuracy of firing from a dynamically moving platform was solved by adopting a high rate of fire, putting a high proportion of projectiles within a given space. As related earlier, General Electric and Philco-Ford were selected to produce hardware for a shoot-off. General Electric had a head start, as it had already

manufactured the definitive American fighter weapon, the M61A 20mm cannon developed for Project 'Vulcan', which had the amazing rate of fire of 6,000 rounds per minute. The M61A was a six-barrel Gatling-type rotary gun, the six barrels allowing a high rate of fire without overheating, as the rate of fire per barrel was only 1,000 rounds per minute; this was slightly more than two-thirds the rate of the latest revolver cannon with but a single barrel.

It was not however a simple matter of scaling up the M61A from 20mm to 30mm calibre. The projectile needed far better ballistic qualities and greater penetrating power than those of the standard 20mm round, even if it were to be scaled up; ammunition for the new gun became the subject of a separate development contract. Although only 50% greater in diameter, the new projectile weighed more than four times as much as the 20mm article.

When a shell is fired, it leaves the barrel at a speed known as the muzzle velocity. In the case of the M61A, this is around 3,400ft/sec, or just over Mach 3, which is close to the limits of that possible with an aircraft gun. To accelerate the larger and much heavier 30mm shell to the same speed, a far greater volume of propellant was needed. Propellant burns at a given rate, creating hot gases, the

Above:
This obsolete M47 tank shows the effects of a gun pass by a Warthog on the firing range. Both turret and hull have been pierced and, most spectacularly, so has the gun barrel. *Fairchild*

Left:
A close-up of the same tank shows the pyrophoric effects of the depleted uranium shell on the driving wheel. *Fairchild*

Above right:
A good idea of the size of the seven-barrel gun rotor is given here by comparison with a pilot's head! *Fairchild*

Right:
The GAU-8/A was mounted aboard a YA-10 and test fired on the ground before air firing tests were initiated. This photo dates from 7 February 1974. *USAF*

pressure of which accelerates the projectile up the barrel, and is released as it leaves the muzzle. It burns at a set rate, and the length of the barrel is determined by the burn time; the greater the amount of propellant, the longer must the barrel be if it is not to be wasted. The barrel length in GAU-8/A is about 80 calibres. Burning propellant also releases heat, and the bigger the charge, the more heat there is to be dissipated. Barrel wear is also a problem: the faster the rate of fire, the greater the rate of wear. A minimum barrel life of 21,000 rounds was called for. To satisfy the heat dissipation and barrel life requirements, the rate of fire was set at 4,200 shells per minute, with a selectable secondary rate of fire of half this, and a seven-barrel rotor was chosen, one barrel more than the M61A. The effect of this was that the GAU-8/A fired at the rate of 10 shells per barrel per second compared with nearly 17 shells per barrel per second by the M61A. Rotary cannon are more reliable than orthodox revolver cannon, because they are externally driven; in the case of GAU-8/A by two hydraulic motors, one from each hydraulic system. This eliminates the most usual cause of stoppages in traditional guns, which is a misfire. As these are powered by the exhaust gases from the ammunition, a misfire deprives the gun of the power to keep it working, whereas with hydraulic drive there is no such problem. In the event of one hydraulic system going inoperative, the other can provide sufficient power to work the rotor, albeit at half the maximum rate of fire. The moving parts of the gun are driven by cams from the rotor, and this has also proved to be more reliable than the reciprocating motion of the traditional cannon. Finally, even when a stoppage occurs, it can often be cleared in flight by reversing the rotor motion, then trying again.

The design burst length was intended to be two seconds, with a one-minute cooling time between bursts. One minute in the target area is a long time, and at first sight this appears to pose a serious operational restriction, but in practice it doesn't work out like this. Test firings of around 10 seconds have been carried out without undue problems. Unlike reciprocating cannon, a rotary type takes time to wind up to full rate — just 0.55

seconds in the case of GAU-8/A. The number of shells fired in the first second is around 50, and trials have shown that a longer burst than this is overkill against most targets, with the result that the 1sec burst has become fairly standardised, and less cooling time is needed. This apart, the usual method of attack is a quick pop-up, aim and fire, then a diving turn back to the cover of the ground. GAU-8/A is well able to hand out destruction in a 1sec burst, followed by a second burst at a target of opportunity if one presents itself during the evasive manoeuvre following the attack.

As is only to be expected, the combination of heavy projectile, high muzzle velocity and high rate of fire produced a considerable recoil, averaging some 10,000lb, or rather more than the maximum static thrust of one of the Warthog's engines. To avoid or minimise the inevitable pitching moment caused when the gun fired, it is aligned 2° downwards in order to point the recoil directly at the aircraft centre of gravity. This has the spin-off effect of reducing the angle of dive necessary to aim by a like amount, which would make a strafing pass at a convoy of vehicles rather easier at low level.

Combat persistence is essential in a dedicated close air support aircraft; as we have seen, this means the survivability to stay in the battle zone, and also the endurance. It also means that the aircraft must carry the munitions to carry out multiple attacks, and this demands an ample supply of gun ammunition. The original requirement was for 10 2sec bursts, or a minimum of 1,200 rounds, which was more than twice the usual capacity of the M61A. This amount, of a far larger shell, needed a large magazine which, as it represented a far more lethal risk in the event of battle damage, had to be well protected. This had a spin-off effect, as we shall see later. The capacity chosen was 1,350 rounds of linkless ammunition stored radially in a helical rotating drum with their bases held in a channel in the fixed outer drum, from whence they are forced into the gun feed chute. Some GAU-8/As have a modified helical rotor which reduces the capacity to 1,174 rounds.

GAU-8/A is enormous, and we can hardly leave it without some reference to its size. The whole assembly is 19.88ft long, the rotor section taking up 9.46ft of this, while the maximum diameter, which occurs at the magazine, is 2.88ft. Empty it weighs 1,963lb, and the full load of ammunition amounts to 2,066lb. Each of the seven barrels weighs 55lb. If you consider these dimensions in relation to the room you are sitting in, and the weights to those of your car, you will understand why a special aircraft had to be built to carry this monster.

In the tank-busting role, the projectile is at least as important as the gun. Penetrating the thick hide of an armoured fighting vehicle is not easy, as the variety of anti-armour weapons currently proliferating testifies. The development of a suitable projectile for the GAU-8/A was at least as difficult, if not more so, than the gun. Shaped charges and other exotic warheads were out, as the necessarily small calibre of the shell would not permit them to be used. This left a kinetic energy penetrator as the only possible choice. The problem became how to transfer the highest possible amount of energy to the smallest possible area of armour.

**The obligatory 'shopping list' is depicted with a
pre-production A-10A. Weapons include AGM-65A
Mavericks, Rockeye cluster bomb dispensers and LGBs.
Many aircraft could match this load until it came to gun
ammunition.** *Fairchild*

The first consideration is muzzle velocity, and
we have already considered the trade-offs of this
when discussing the design of the gun. The next
factor is the ballistic qualities. The projectile is
travelling at its maximum velocity (speed) as it
leaves the muzzle, after which it progressively
slows down due to aerodynamic drag, and as it
slows, its kinetic energy bleeds off. As the formula
for kinetic energy is $\frac{1}{2}v^2 \times$ mass, it can be seen that
velocity (v) is very important. A good ballistic
shape is therefore essential to minimise drag, and
with it, speed loss.

Mass is also important; the projectile needs to
be heavy to maximise the kinetic energy, and this
raises the question of what materials to use. Where
the shell is to be HEI (High Explosive Incendiary),
the need to produce a fragmenting warhead with a
quantity of explosive within it, plus a fuse in the
nose, reduces the options. A practice round
requires the cheapest material of the correct
weight that will reproduce the flight conditions of
the 'real' round accurately. Armour piercing (AP)
is another matter.

The traditional AP round relies on tungsten for
penetration. This is a heavy and hard metal which,
alloyed with steel, gives good penetration qualities. It is fairly expensive. There is however
something rather better, at one-eighth of the price,
readily available, and almost completely useless
for anything else other than ballast. This is the
element U238, or depleted uranium. Cheapness
apart, DU (as it is commonly known) has two
tremendous advantages. Firstly it is extremely
heavy, being 60% denser than lead. Second, it is a
pyrophoric material which ignites on impact,
adding fire to its penetrative qualities. Of course,
all armour-piercing rounds glow red on impact; the
kinetic energy has to go somewhere, and it is
released in the form of heat. But DU is something
else; it actually ignites, rather than just releasing
the stored energy, and is thus potentially far more
lethal.

The decision to use DU was a bold one; the
word uranium conjures up visions of nuclear
weapons, with all the attendant hazards of
radiation. Predictably, the Soviet Union fulmi-
nated about the use of what they termed 'nuclear
bullets', although this was quite unjustified. The
nasty element is actually Uranium 235; U238 is a
byproduct of the U235 extraction process and has
only a residual amount of radiation, rather less
than that emitted by the average luminous watch
dial. There are in fact two dangers arising from use
of a DU projectile. The first is that machining it

gives rise to the highly toxic uranium oxide, which can be negated by strict manufacturing controls. The second is if a weapons loader drops it on his toe! We are of course talking about accidental dangers.

It is not widely realised that uranium shells have been around for some considerable time, Hitler's Germany having used the substance in tank shells from 1943, when tungsten supplies ran short.

In the event, three different types of shell were produced for the GAU-8/A. They were the PGU-14/B API (Armour Piercing Incendiary); the PGU-13/B HEI; and the PGU-15/B TP or practice round. While the dimensions remained constant — they had to, to fit the chamber, at 11.42in long — the weights and muzzle velocities all varied. The API shell weighed 727g, with a projectile weight of 425g and a muzzle velocity of 3,225ft/sec, compared with the HEI, which was 662g, 360g, and 3,350ft/sec; and the TP, with 667g, 365g, and 3,340ft/sec respectively. The API consisted of a DU core roughly 15mm in diameter, held in an aluminium base and with an aluminium nose shield. The advantage of this arrangement was that the point of impact, where most of the energy lies, is reduced to a quarter of that taken up by a 30mm shell. The core, which acts as a penetrator, is an alloy of DU with a small percentage of titanium added as a hardener. The difference in shell weights and muzzle velocities of the different types is due entirely to the differing projectile weights, the case and the propellant charge being identical in all cases.

Two points that are common to all three types of shell are that they all use an aluminium cartridge

BAU-1/A Shells

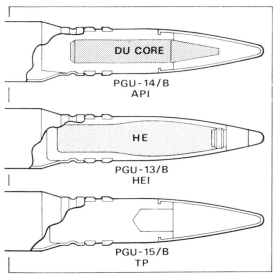

PGU-14/B API

PGU-13/B HEI

PGU-15/B TP

PGU-14/B API

Round length	290mm
Round weight	727g
Projectile weight	425g
Muzzle velocity	982m/sec (3,225ft/sec)

PGU-13/B HEI

Round length	290mm
Round weight	662g
Projectile weight	360g
Muzzle velocity	1,021m/sec (3,350ft/sec)

PGU-15/B TP

Round length	290mm
Round weight	667g
Projectile weight	365g
Muzzle velocity	1,018m/sec (3,340ft/sec)

Ballistics Comparison

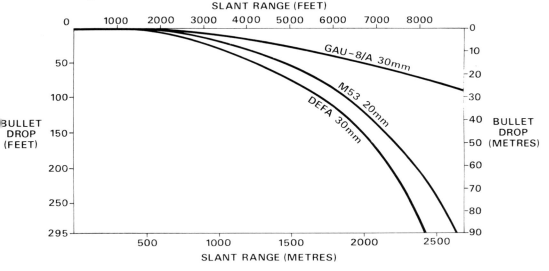

Above:
In this eight-picture sequence, a 'full up' M48 tank was used as a target for an A-10A gun attack. M48s were found to be slightly less resistant than the Soviet T-62 main battle tank. *Fairchild*

Right:
Maverick missiles with electro-optical guidance are the primary weapon of the A-10A. The second pre-production aircraft is shown making an early test launch. *Fairchild*

case, which was adopted as a weight-saving measure and is the first production application of this type in a high performance gun; and the use of plastic rotating bands on the projectile instead of the more traditional copper, which not only saves weight and cost, but also barrel wear by an amount calculated to increase barrel life threefold.

Much has been written about the accuracy of the GAU-8/A and the API projectile. The accuracy requirement was 80% shot dispersion within 5 mils, a mil being the angle subtended by an object 1ft long at a distance of 1,000ft, which equals 0.057°. In trials, an accuracy of 80% within 4 mils has been achieved. Maximum range for effective shooting is about 6,000ft, and the time of flight of the projectile is just about two seconds. At the optimum anti-armour range of 4,000ft, the time of flight is just 1.2 seconds, during which any vehicle more than 12ft long travelling at 20mph would not move more than its own length.

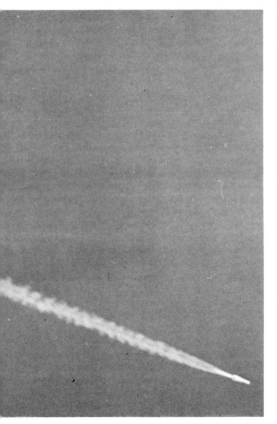

Shooting, even at a deflection angle of 90°, would not require any aim-off under these conditions, and would for all practical purposes be point-blank. How effective the gun would be against the latest composite armours is debatable in terms of penetration, but the chances of a disabling or immobilising hit must be very high. Compared to the 20mm projectile of the M61A, the 3½ times heavier 30mm article carries a much heavier punch with far greater accuracy. Using a dive angle of 15° at a speed of 350kt, and firing from an altitude of 4,000ft, the 30mm projectile suffers a drop of some 10 mils at a slant range of about 7,000ft, compared to the 20mm weapon which achieves this level of inaccuracy at a slant range of barely 4,500ft.

Although the A-10A was designed around the massive GAU-8/A, this is no longer considered to be its primary weapon. That honour now goes to the AGM-65 Maverick, a guided weapon developed by the Hughes Aircraft Co. Maverick, the first of which was handed over to the USAF as far back as August 1972, can be used by a variety of aircraft, not just the Warthog, and comes in many different forms, using TV, laser and IIR guidance. Aerodynamically it owes much to the AIM-4 Falcon by the same company.

From the sort of speeds and altitudes that the A-10A is likely to launch Maverick (low and slow), the missile has a theoretical range of 6-7nm, but in practice it is difficult to get the seeker to lock on at more than 2nm. This is still far enough to give the Warthog a useful stand-off capability, which is

sorely needed as modern defences improve. The fact that it is a launch-and-leave weapon adds greatly to its value.

The Maverick types typically carried by the A-10A are the AGM-65B, which has scene magnification televisual guidance; and, since mid-1986, the AGM-65D, which uses IIR (imaging infra-red). In each case, lock-on is achieved by contrast, either light against dark or vice versa in the visible light spectrum, or hot against cold in infra-red, which of course shows up as light and dark on the cockpit display. The procedure for launch is as follows: the pilot selects a Maverick and a light in the cockpit indicates when it is ready. The 'uncage' switch then removes a protective cover from the nose of the missile, and the seeker head then displays what it can see on to a screen in the cockpit. The pilot then acquires a target, pulls up briefly and aligns the target in his gunsight. It should then appear on the screen display, and cross hairs on the screen are fine-tuned on to the target. Maverick can then be launched, and needs no further assistance from the A-10A, which is free to turn away.

Maverick has an operational kill record of 88%; early versions were used experimentally in South-East Asia, while the Israeli Air Force obtained excellent results with the AGM-65A in the October War of 1973.

The AGM-65D IIR Maverick has a greater ability to penetrate dust and smoke, and can to a degree discriminate between different types of vehicles due to their IR signature. It can also be used at night, although it is unable to see through fog or rain. Its better discrimination allows it to be used to attack a radar that has just been switched off, the missile homing on the heat still being emitted, a handy attribute against mobile radar-controlled battlefield weapons. The superior discrimination allows stand-off ranges to be doubled, an advantage of inestimable value against an opponent equipped with modern air defence weapons. A, B and D Mavericks all employ a warhead weighing 125lb containing a forward

Anti-Armour Kill Potential

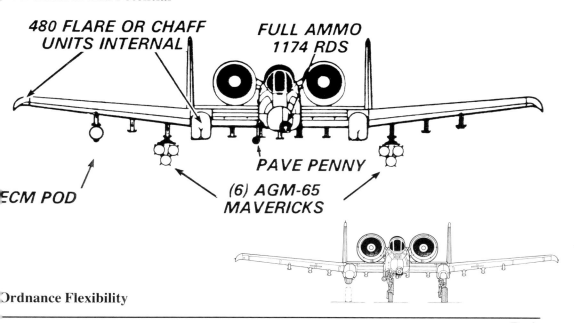

480 FLARE OR CHAFF UNITS INTERNAL

FULL AMMO 1174 RDS

PAVE PENNY

ECM POD

(6) AGM-65 MAVERICKS

Ordnance Flexibility

Store	kg		11	10	9	8	7	6	5	4	3	2	1	Total max
Mk 82 LDGP — General Purpose Bomb	240	(*529)	1	1	3	3	6	6	6	3	3	1	1	28
Mk 82 HDGP — General Purpose Bomb	249	(549)	1	1	3	3	6	6	6	3	3	1	1	28
Mk 84 LDGP — General Purpose Bomb	894	(1,971)	—	—	1	1	1	1	1	1	1	—	—	6
BLU-27 A/B, B/B, C/B (UF) Fire Bomb	362	(798)	—	1	2	1	1	—	1	1	2	1	—	11
BLU-27 A/B, B/B, C/B (F) Fire Bomb	369	(813)	—	1	2	1	1	—	1	1	2	1	—	10
SUU-25 C/A Flare Dispenser	224	(494)	—	1	3	—	—	—	—	—	3	1	—	8
LAU-68 A/A Rocket Launcher	110	(243)	—	1	3	3	3	3	3	3	3	1	—	20
LAU-68 B/A Rocket Launcher	120	(265)	—	1	3	3	3	3	3	3	3	1	—	20
Mk 36 Mod 1, 2, 3 Destructor Bomb	254	(560)	1	1	3	3	6	6	6	3	3	1	1	28
BLU-52 A/B, B, Riot Control Bomb	159	(351)	—	1	2	1	1	—	1	1	2	1	—	11
Mk 20 Mod 3 (Rockeye II) Dispenser	216	(476)	1	1	3	3	6	6	6	3	3	1	1	28
CBU-58/B Dispenser SUU-30	372	(820)	1	1	3	2	2	6	2	2	3	1	1	20
CBU-71/B Dispenser SUU-30	372	(820)	1	1	3	2	2	6	2	2	3	1	1	20
CBU-52 A/B, B, B/B Dispenser SUU-30	356	(785)	1	1	3	2	2	6	2	2	3	1	1	20
AGM-65/A Maverick Missile	210	(463)	—	—	3	—	—	—	—	—	3	—	—	6
SUU-23A 20mm Gun Pod	789	(1,739)	—	—	—	—	1	—	1	—	—	—	—	2
Mk 82 Laser Bomb GBU-12/B, A/B	295	(650)	1	—	1	1	—	—	—	1	1	—	1	6
Mk 84 Laser Bomb GBU-10/B, A/B, B/B	934	(2,059)	—	—	1	1	—	—	—	1	1	—	—	4
Mk 84 EO — TV-Guided Bomb GBU-8/B	1,027	(2,264)	—	—	1	1	—	—	—	1	1	—	—	4
SUU-20A, A/A, A/M, B/A, Training Dispenser	125	(276)	—	—	—	1	1	—	1	1	—	—	—	4
BDU-33B, A/B, B/B — Practice Bomblet	11	(24)	—	—	3	3	6	6	6	3	3	—	—	24
ECM Pod (AN/ALQ-119)	249	(549)	1	—	—	—	—	—	—	—	—	1	—	2
600gal Fuel Tank	1,887	(4,160)	—	—	—	1	—	1	—	1	—	—	—	3
AIM-9L Sidewinder	85	(188)	2	—	—	—	—	—	—	—	—	—	2	4
MER-10N — Multiple Ejector Rack	100	(220)	—	—	—	—	1	1	1	—	—	—	—	3
TER-9A — Triple Ejector Rack	42	(93)	—	—	1	1	1	1	1	1	1	—	—	6
LAU-88/A Maverick Launcher — Triple	210	(463)	—	—	1	—	—	—	—	—	1	—	—	2

Other Weapons:

CBU-72B
BLY-95B } Fuel Air Explosive Weapon
BLU-96B

Weights in lbs in parentheses

Above:
The last moments of an M48 main battle tank, as an AGM-65A homes in. Homing is set on contrast, which here can be seen to be good, the dark tank showing up well against the lighter ground.
Hughes Missile Division

Centre:
With decelerons deployed to stabilise the speed in a dive, an A-10A launches a Maverick on the Edwards test range. USAF

Left:
The first A-10A unit to become operational with IIR Maverick was the 91st TFS, based at Woodbridge, in May 1986.
Hughes Missile Division

firing conical-shaped charge, with very good penetration qualities, which is excellent against armour.

The Warthog is often depicted with a huge load of ordnance slung beneath its wings, or an impressive variety of stores displayed in front of it, and one might be forgiven for thinking that dropping bombs is its main function. While the A-10A is no slouch in the conventional bombing mode — during trials it achieved an average error of 13.6 mils, which was rather better than the 15 mils called for — few of the stores that it is cleared to carry are likely to be used in action. While the maximum load of 28 Mk 82 slicks looks impressive, it demands a considerable length of hard runway from which to operate, and forces the A-10A to revert to the vulnerable dive-attack mode. The most likely free-fall weapons to be used are laser-guided bombs of the Paveway series or, under certain circumstances, cluster bomb units such as the Rockeye II LG CBU, which contains some 200 hollow charge bomblets of 2.1in diameter. Laser guidance was not incorporated originally, but was an 'add-on', in the form of the Pave Penny laser target seeker pod which is carried on a special pylon on the right of the forward fuselage just beneath the cockpit. Pave Penny has other uses, as we shall see later.

As defences get stronger and the A-10A gets older, further attempts are being made to give it a stand-off tank-killing capability at less cost than Maverick. The most promising at present is Vought's HVM, or Hypervelocity Missile. Rocket propelled, this is designed with a solid warhead for a kinetic energy kill. Just 3.8in in diameter, it is many times heavier than the API shell of the GAU-8/A, and also travels much faster, attaining speeds exceeding 5,000ft/sec, around Mach 4.5. The fire control system consists of a forward-looking infra-red sensor for target acquisition and tracking, and a carbon dioxide laser for steering. The first flight tests took place at White Sands Missile Range in 1983, when the HVM proved its impulsive thrust control system, attained the required speeds, and demonstrated its ability to receive steering commands from the laser through its exhaust plume. Further tests are scheduled for late 1987, which will include multiple launches at multiple targets.

The final weapon to be carried is the AIM-9L Sidewinder, which has been undergoing trials. Up to four can be carried on dual rail adapters on the outboard wing stations; they will give the Warthog a credible air-to-air capability for self defence. The slow but manoeuvrable A-10A is a difficult target at low level at the best of times, and Sidewinder will make an air defence fighter more cautious before attacking, as the tables can be quickly turned when he overshoots.

The A-10A, with its rapid turn-round capability and simple systems, makes heavy demands on the armament groundcrews. Tech Sgt Bruce Christopherson is an armament systems technician, usually called a weaponeer, currently with the 81st TFW at Bentwaters. Prior to this assignment he spent four years as an A-10 weapons instructor at

the USAF technical school, and also had two years working on the A-10 at Davis-Monthan AFB. Here he talks about his work:

'We work as a crew of three, usually all male but sometimes we have a female on the crew. It's no big deal. The first thing we do is to go out to the aircraft and determine from the flying schedule what the munitions for the next mission will be. If you are talking wartime missions, you really have only two primary munitions: Maverick and the gun. Let's take the gun first.

'Usually a separate crew loads the gun, and another the bombs or missiles. Loading the gun calls for a special apparatus called the ALS, or Automatic Loading System. It can load about 300 rounds per minute. The crew can arrive at the aircraft, hook all their equipment up, position their trailers with the ammunition on them, and connect them, and start feeding the aircraft. If they are good they can get done in 20 minutes, and that includes offloading the expended cases at the same time.

'Gun maintenance is pretty easy. The barrels don't need cleaning because the rotating bands on the projectiles are plastic, so there is no debris left in the barrel after firing, just powder residue. It cleans itself every time it fires. The gun is very reliable, and has no specific troubles, but you have to realise that we fire thousands and thousands of rounds every week. A lot of inspections are required before the gun system can be used, and

we run dummy rounds through just to make sure everything works properly.

'A major facet of our work here is troubleshooting the gun. It takes a lot of experience, and we only have a few people qualified to do it. Usually it's just a piece breaks through fatigue due to the thousands of rounds that are fired. Another cause is sometimes faulty ammunition. The rotor turns so quickly that if you get a round which has a slow burning primer it fails to fire in time. The round is extracted, and explodes outside the gun, or sometimes it makes it back to the container for the empties. All that happens is that the aluminium case explodes and small pieces of ali [aluminium] fly about. There is debris everywhere, and it jams the gun, which just stops automatically. It is always contained; I have never seen an aircraft damaged by this cause, and the projectile itself doesn't try to go anywhere. Then we have to remove the gun and find the cause of the stoppage.

'I have probably done a thousand complete

removals and installations of the gun system in my
time with the A-10. It's easy when you have done it
a lot, but it can be difficult for a person who has
never worked on the aircraft before, and is not
used to handling large pieces of gear that have to
go into a small space, and there are a lot of pieces
involved. It is repetitious; the more you do it, the
faster you get, and the less problems with the
systems you have.

'Early in the service life of the aircraft there was
a programme called "Lead the Fleet". Three or
four aircraft on every base were selected to fire
their guns at the rate of 1,000 rounds per day for
every day of the flying week. They fired them until
they jammed, then pulled them out and examined
them, and only replaced the things that actually
broke, to see how long the stuff would last. That's
how they came up with the intervals for changing
things. Take the barrels. We keep track of how
many rounds have been fired, and change them at
set intervals, no matter how good they might look.
We've got a gun borescope which we stick down
the barrel to check for pitting and erosion, which
we do when the gun is removed for maintenance,
but we still change the barrels at the set intervals.

'To load Maverick we use what is called a bomb
lift truck, a bit like a fork lift truck. We do our
inspections to make sure there is nothing wrong
with the missile, then there are two ways of loading
it. You can load the missile on to a launcher and
then put the launcher on the aircraft, or put the

launcher on first, then load the missiles. After
putting the launcher on, you set the switches in the
cockpit. When handling Maverick, you earth
yourself constantly, as the main hazard is static
discharge, which could fire the rocket motor. Of
course, all munitions have to be handled carefully.

'For other missions you might have GP bombs.
If there is a heavy load, it takes a little more time,
because you have to bring each bomb in, lock it up
and put a pin in it, one at a time until they are all
positioned, then make sure all the fuses are set
properly, cut any wires that need it, then finally
insert the explosive charges that make the bombs
fall off the airplane.

'Integrated combat is one thing we do quite
often. Basically we don't practice, because we are
loading the airplane with weapons all the time, but
this we do practice because it is realistic. We have
to do the whole thing in full chemical gear,
complete with gas mask. It's hot; if it's 85°F you
still have to wear this thing, and the sweat just
pours off you. As it has got nowhere to go, it just
stays inside your mask. Loading the airplane under
these conditions, and trying to use manual
dexterity while wearing heavy gloves, is not easy,
but we still have to do it within a specified time,
and safely, otherwise we have to come back the
next day and try again.

'You notice as you go from base to base that
each has its own requirements. At Davis-Monthan
we were working for pilot training, while here we

re ready for war. At Bentwaters we load practice bombs most of the time, then we what we call generate" with the real thing. You never know hen it is going to come. It came on a Saturday ight when I was in Germany. The weather was ad; 20°F below, freezing rain, and a gale blowing. Under those conditions your hands don't work so ell, and that can be a problem. Most of what we o you need to have your hands free; gloves are oo bulky and get in the way.'

We have examined the aircraft, we have examined the weapons. What is their worth? Studies made in 1978 showed that the kill potential per sortie of the A-10A was no less than 7.0 AFVs. By comparison, the F-4, A-7 and F-16 rated at 2.4, while the French Jaguar scored 0.8 and the Mirage F.1 a miserable 0.6. The only remaining doubt is survivability. In part this is a hardware reaction, but the rest is down to the mission and tactics, which we shall examine in the next chapter.

bove left:
oading a big gun on a big aircraft a big job, and it needs a big achine to do it. This is the Hydra utomatic loader.
rank Mormillo

bove:
bomb hoist is used to load a k 80 on to an A-10A of the 354th FW at Myrtle Beach. *USAF*

ight:
orking in NBC kit complicates e for the groundcrews. Not even e ANG units are exempt from ese exercises; this is the 104th FG from Michigan. *USAF*

Top:
The completed N/AW A-10 is seen here finished in gunship grey, with a long-range tank on the centreline.
Fairchild

Above:
Practice weapons loaded, this 81st TFW machine prepares to taxi out as the groundcrew, wearing ear protectors against the noise, make final checks.
Mike Ryan

Below:
December 1980, and a factory-fresh A-10A of the 104th TFG rolls out after landing at Indian Springs.
Frank Mormillo

Bottom:
Many paint schemes were tried out in the JAWS evaluation using various colour spots and lozenges. This 57th FWW machine, seen at Nellis, was just one example. *Frank Mormillo*

5 Mission & Tactics

The A-10A Thunderbolt II has been the object of a tremendous amount of criticism from its inception, much of it ill-informed, and often from those who ought to know better. The controversy stems basically from the slow operational speed, and the survivability measures incorporated in design, which, let's face it, are rather extraordinary. The argument against the A-10A goes thus: the best way to survive over the battlefield is not to be hit, and fast jets survive in this arena because their speed only gives the enemy air defences a fleeting time in which to shoot at them. Any air defence system takes a finite time to acquire the target, track it, predict its course and speed, and launch a projectile, either guided or unguided, at it.

This proposition is unarguable, but it does tend to be misleading, as it seems to imply that *only* a fast jet can survive over the battlefield. Many

Exploiting Air Defence System Limitations: ZSU-23/4

The diagram indicates the potential aiming error of the ZSU-23/4 linear predictor computer against a manoeuvring A-10A.

commentators have taken this view in the past, but how many of them have also decried the use of the battlefield helicopter, which is even slower than the A-10A? There is an anomaly here which is very relevant to the role of the Warthog.

Let us briefly return to basics. Just as there is no free lunch, so there is no free shot in warfare. Any aircraft, regardless of how fast it is, will get shot at; whether by missiles or by guns is irrelevant. The amount of fire put up against it will depend on a number of factors: how much warning of its approach it will give; the number of counter-air weapons in that particular locality, and their capability; and, most important of all, the number of weapons that just happen to be pointing in roughly the right direction at the right time. Speed is not the ultimate arbiter: the window open to the counter-air defences is determined by a combination of high speed and low altitude. There is also a limit to this combination which is set by the pilot of the fast jet: how fast and low can he fly and still perform his assigned mission? If he can fly fast enough low enough for long enough to survive over the battlefield but is unable to carry out his task, he would be better off having stayed at home. High speed is also counter-productive in taking evasive action; turn radius is a function of speed,

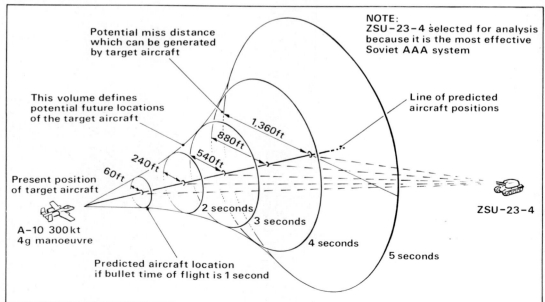

Potential miss distance which can be generated by target aircraft

NOTE:
ZSU-23-4 selected for analysis because it is the most effective Soviet AAA system

This volume defines potential future locations of the target aircraft

Line of predicted aircraft positions

1,360ft

880ft

540ft

240ft

60ft

Present position of target aircraft

A-10 300kt
4g manoeuvre

2 seconds

3 seconds

4 seconds

5 seconds

ZSU-23-4

Predicted aircraft location if bullet time of flight is 1 second

Maverick Stand-off Missile Attack Profile

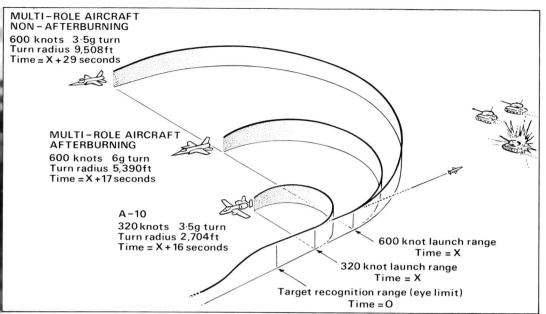

MULTI-ROLE AIRCRAFT
NON-AFTERBURNING

600 knots 3·5g turn
Turn radius 9,508ft
Time = X + 29 seconds

MULTI-ROLE AIRCRAFT
AFTERBURNING

600 knots 6g turn
Turn radius 5,390ft
Time = X + 17 seconds

A-10
320 knots 3·5g turn
Turn radius 2,704ft
Time = X + 16 seconds

600 knot launch range
Time = X

320 knot launch range
Time = X

Target recognition range (eye limit)
Time = O

Sustained Manoeuvre Performance

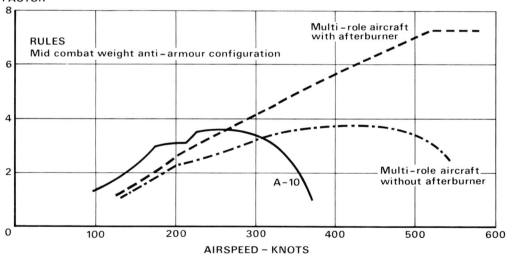

NORMAL
LOAD FACTOR

RULES
Mid combat weight anti-armour configuration

Multi-role aircraft
with afterburner

A-10

Multi-role aircraft
without afterburner

AIRSPEED – KNOTS

and the larger the radius and slower the rate of turn, the more the fast jet is predictable, and therefore vulnerable. Finally, there is no certainty in war; Mars has a warped sense of humour at times, and having accepted that any aircraft over the battlefield is going to get shot at, it goes without saying that occasionally it will be hit, and that sometimes the hit will be lethal.

Having said all that about fast jets, the inference is often drawn that a slow jet, such as the Warthog, must certainly be hit on every sortie, and at least one commentator has painted a lurid picture of every A-10A being grounded by massive damage after the first morning in action, and having to sit out the rest of the conflict on their airfields in varying states of disrepair.

Above right:
The Vietnam experience gave rise to the A-X requirement which resulted in the A-10A. The forests of Connecticut give a passable imitation of South-East Asia to this overflying 103rd TFG aircraft. *USAF*

Top:
A pre-production aircraft rolls away from the T-37 chase plane for a strafing attack on M48 and T-62 tanks. The star and bar under the starboard wing appears to have been stuck on back to front, so modellers looking for an excuse. . . ! *Fairchild*

Right:
Forward basing, carrying light loads out of semi-prepared strips, is part of the A-10A operational philosophy, in order to reduce the reaction time when a call comes.
Fairchild via Mike Ryan

This is untrue for a variety of reasons. The use of stand-off weapons — and the gun should be included because it far out-ranges the ZSU-23/4 Shilka — coupled with slow flight and extreme manoeuvrability, will ensure that the A-10A, like the fast jet, is only exposed to hostile fire for a very brief period, and its slowness will enable it to use terrain masking in a way that the fast jet can hardly ever do. It should be remembered here that terrain masking is the chief survival feature of the battlefield helicopter, and the A-10A also uses it, although to a lesser degree, and it remains an important factor in avoiding being hit. Finally, while an occasional hit is inevitable, the survivability features of the A-10A will often allow it to return to base in circumstances where a less well protected aircraft would be lost. There it can be repaired; or, if the damage is too heavy, it will constitute a valuable source of spare parts for the other aircraft in the unit. A further consideration is that the CAS mission is a particularly fatiguing one, being flown almost entirely at low level, with no assistance from an autopilot (none is fitted), and with navigation done by map and stopwatch in

the main, coupled with familiarity with the area of operations. The pilot-to-aircraft ratio in Warthog squadrons is higher than average due to this factor; the aircraft can fly considerably more missions than a pilot during the course of a day, and even in an A-10A returned in a catastrophically shot-up state, the irreplaceable pilot would be saved.

The basic point remains that the A-10A is not as easy a target for the opposing defences as it has often been represented, and the mission profile and tactics adopted will be tailored to maximise this aspect. It should also be remembered that even in a 'worst case' Central European scenario it will not be Warthogs against the opposing flak, SAMs, and fighters, but *all* friendly air and counter-air units against *all* hostile air and counter-air units, which is a totally different ball game. The combination of the parts is far greater than the sum total of the individual elements; confusion will become a player that will benefit the side that is best trained, most flexible and has the most suitable equipment.

Even as the Warthog was entering service, the threat was changing, invalidating the original mission concept. For the CAS mission, speed of reaction to assist beleaguered ground forces was deemed to be essential, and this could be achieved in one of two ways. The first was to loiter in a holding area near the battle zone for an extended period, forming a 'cab rank' from which aircraft

Below:
An A-10A of the 57th FWW hauls hard right off the runway at Nellis during a 'Red Flag' exercise in 1980.
USAF

The Use of Terrain Masking

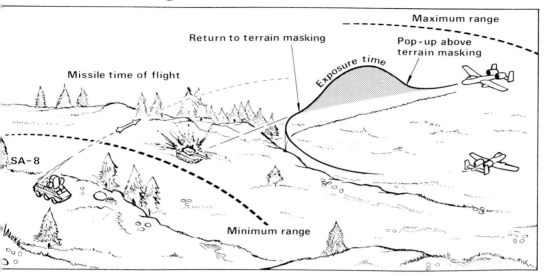

uld be drawn as needed; while the second was forward basing, operating from semi-prepared strips fairly close behind the FLOT. In the first case, a typical mission profile would be to take-off from a permanent base loaded with full internal but no external fuel, 750 rounds for the gun and 18 Mk 82 low drag 500lb bombs, climb out to 20,000ft, then cruise at 227kt true air speed (TAS) for a distance of roughly 125nm before climbing to 25,000ft and increasing the TAS to 300kt. Once in the area, some 250nm from base, the A-10As would descend to 5,000ft and loiter there until called upon, for a duration of up to two hours. Once assigned a target, 10 minutes at full throttle was allowed for a series of attacks, followed by a climb-out to 25,000ft and an economic cruise back to base at 250kt TAS. If all had gone according to plan, enough fuel would remain for 20 minutes loiter at 150kt. Alternatively, forward basing could be used to give what amounted to a permanent loiter capability close to the FLOT. With the gross take-off weight reduced to 30,000lb by the simple expedient of reducing the internal fuel to 4,225lb (550 US gal) and the bombload to four Mk 82s, the Warthog could be off the ground after a roll of just 1,000ft, fly 50nm to the combat area, spend 30 minutes at full throttle in the attack, then return to base with the same fuel margin as in the first case.

It is noticeable that gun ammunition had been reduced to save weight, and that the other weapon carried was the old-fashioned 'iron' bomb. The A-10A had achieved excellent bombing results on the range, the delivery being made at moderate dive angle at a stabilised speed, and begun from a medium to low altitude. The outstanding accuracy was due to a very short slant range from the release

point to the target which reduced many of the aiming and trajectory problems encountered during a similar attack by a fast jet. The gun attack, as practiced, involved acquiring the target on the first pass, turning tightly to keep the target in view, then attacking it on the second time around. These methods would be perfectly feasible in the counter-insurgency mission, against a limited enemy defensive capability, but the rather leisurely attack modes depicted would have increased the time that the A-10A was visible to the enemy gunners or missileers, with a corresponding increase in the probability of being hit. Meanwhile, the Soviet Union had been both increasing and improving its air defence weapons, and the ability of the Warthog to survive in the 'worst case' European scenario was increasingly called into question.

While the A-10A possessed a high degree of resistance to hits from the standard 20mm and 23mm guns, and also the shoulder-fired SA-7 'Grail', new Soviet weapons were entering service that were even more deadly. Chief among these were the ZSU-23/4 'Shilka' self-propelled gun, the highly mobile SA-8 'Gecko' and the MiG-23 'Flogger'.

The 'Shilka' was a quadruple-barrelled radar-laid gun, mounted on a tracked AFV chassis, and was intended to accompany the main battle tanks and protect them against air attack. A very accurate and rapid firing weapon, it tends to chew up an aircraft like a buzz-saw, with multiple hits. It first came to prominence in the October War of 1973, until which time its lethality had not been fully appreciated. The main weakness was range, its effectiveness falling away past around 3,300ft,

75

Left:
Low vis matt paint is all very well, but the effect is rather spoilt by the bright TAC and unit markings, also by the red diagonal on the fin of this 356th TFS, 354th TFW machine seen at Myrtle Beach in November 1981. *Robert Shaw*

Below:
The 'hippie headband' and white outlined tail codes on this 81st TFW aircraft are definitely non-standard. *Peter Foster*

Bottom:
The outboard split airbrakes are shown to advantage by this aircraft of the 343rd TFW landing at Nellis AFB during 'Gunsmoke 85'. *Frank Mormillo*

which meant that it was considerably out-ranged
by the GAU-8/A. On the other hand, the pilot has
to know it is there to avoid getting within its lethal
envelope. Next came the SA-8 'Gecko', a large
and potent missile system carried in batteries of
six, and highly mobile, with both radar and
electro-optical tracking, and a warhead of sufficient size to make survivability measures a purely
academic consideration. 'Gecko' made its public
debut in the Red Square parade of 7 November
1975.

Both the aforegoing weapons increased the risk
in the battle area; but the third, the MiG-23
'Flogger', was a counter-air fighter being built in
enormous numbers. No longer could the West
assume a measure of air superiority over its own
side of the lines; while 'Flogger' was not exactly
the sort of fighter that one would *choose* to go to
war in, its speed combined with advanced radar,
weaponry and, above all, sheer numbers, made the
whole concept of loitering for hours just behind
the lines at 5,000ft a very questionable under-
taking, as well as casting doubt on the wisdom of
medium to high altitude transits to and from the
battle area.

Right:
**A tanker's-eye view of the Warthog will be a small
angular shape in the distance, if he sees it at all, while a
ZSU-23/4 'Shilka' crew would be lucky to get a view as
good as this, skylined and fairly close in.** *USAF*

Below:
**The 354th TFW gets its first Mavericks. False canopies
can just be made out painted on the nose gear doors.**
General Electric

Yet a fourth factor entered the equation, with the increasing use of electronic countermeasures by the Soviet forces. A holding area behind the lines with a bunch of Warthogs flying around in circles waiting for their call would be of little use if the call failed to get through. This factor also cast doubts about the effectiveness of forward basing. The A-10A, with its on-board APU, could generate its own power and keep its communications kit operative even with the engines not running, but if jamming blotted out the radios, they might as well not be there. Forward basing was only feasible if the communications were secure.

The result was that the A-10A mission concept was re-thought. Maverick replaced the bomb as a main Warthog weapon, and gave a worthwhile stand-off capability. Tactics were revised, and a low altitude transit to and from the target area adopted; and instead of the cab-rank system, the fire hose principle was adopted of a continuous supply of aircraft being pointed to where they were most needed at any given moment. At the same time a combined arms approach was instituted, the essence of which was the old established practice that the whole is greater than the sum of the parts. The idea was to integrate the firepower and overall effect of artillery, battlefield helicopters and A-10As, and was operationally assessed in a series of exercises in the late 1970s under the title of Joint Attack Weapons Systems, a rather contrived-sounding name which gives the acronym of JAWS. The underlying concept was that different targets require different weapon systems, and a modern battlefield contains a lot of different targets. JAWS led to the Joint Air Attack Team (JAAT), which is now official doctrine. A high level of co-ordination is needed, and this is provided through Air Support Operations Centers, linked to Army brigade commanders.

The first link in the chain is provided by the artillery field batteries, or sometimes even mortar

Above:
The figures of groundcrew give scale to the huge fighter. From this angle, the amount of offset of the nose gear leg is very visible.
Mike Ryan

Left:
An 81st TFW aircraft seen in its hardened shelter at Bentwaters.
Mike Ryan

platoons. Reconnaissance helicopters are responsible for locating the enemy formation and calling down fire from the guns, at the same time getting the attack helicopters into position. The target priorities are anti-aircraft guns, mobile SAMs and only then command vehicles if they can be located. A secondary purpose of the artillery barrage is to force the tank crews to 'button up', which considerably reduces their effectiveness. Meanwhile, the attack helos move into ambush positions, and the Warthogs are called in. The proceedings are choreographed by one or more Forward Air Controllers (FACs) either on the ground or heliborne; or in extreme circumstances the FAC can be in an A-10A, using two of the three A-10A radios (VHF-AM and VHF-FM) which are standard to the United States Army. All this of course depends on the lack of enemy comm-jamming.

Several tactical innovations came out of the JAWS exercises. The Warthog driver has to visually identify his target; this was not necessarily provided by the FAC, who generally gave an IP for the pop-up from which the pilot could pick his own target. The ingress was made at low level, the rule being that the helicopters operated below tree-top level and the A-10As above it. Smoke and flame from the battle area often provided good visual cues on the run-in; but, oddly enough, so did the friendly helicopters which, as they were not often masked from the rear, could easily be seen. If they were at the hover, or moving slowly forward, it was a reasonable assumption that they were normally facing the enemy, and about 10,000ft away. The A-10As hunted in pairs, but the abreast and trail formations were found to be too inflexible. Simultaneous attacks or closely co-ordinated attacks were found to be the most effective, with the runs being made between 20° and 30° off line. With the attacking pilots having to concentrate on visually acquiring their targets and then aiming accurately, it was found essential to make pilots coming off the target after an attack responsible for collision avoidance.

The most 'front line' Warthog outfit is the 81st TFW based at RAF Bentwaters and RAF Woodbridge in England. This wing is numerically the largest in the entire USAF, with a total of six squadrons of 18 aircraft each. It also has four Forward Operating Locations (FOLs) in Germany, at Ahlhorn, Norvenich, Sembach and Leipheim, all of which are roughly 100nm in from the East German/Czechoslovakian border, and to which the squadrons of the 81st frequently deploy as part of their training schedule. Lt-Col Robert J. Burke USAF is the Assistant Deputy Commander, Operations, at Bentwaters, and before this assignment commanded the 91st TFS at Woodbridge. His thoughts on the operational employment of the A-10A at war have therefore a very special relevance. He is, like all pilots who fly the Warthog, an enthusiast.

'I think a lot of the criticisms of the airplane depend on people's perspectives, and on what sort of scenario they want to concoct. I guess that is where it has taken the worst flak. Personally I think that we can be very, very effective, but the bottom line is that we don't know for certain what the scenario will be, or how the airplane will be used.

'A typical scenario is a very heavily armoured invasion, with motorised rifle regiments leading, a blitzkreig type approach. I think we could be very effective if we were put in on the front end of that to slow it up, and force the supporting echelons to back up. I think we can buy time for the follow-up forces to get here, but munitions are the problem; Gen Rogers wrote in *Stars and Stripes* the other day, and he says we only have enough weapons to last a matter of days. But of course, in a conventional war, the whole theatre is a problem for supplies of weapons. But if we did get a Warpac invasion of Central Europe, I think this airplane is going to be extremely effective in slowing them down, and knocking them off their game plan.

'A lot depends where the main thrust comes. Up in the North German plain, around Hamburg and wherever, there aren't a lot of hills. It's like the American mid-West, you'd get a tank division rolling up there in pretty good shape. Down South, in the Fulda Gap region, we've got a much better terrain to work over; this particular airplane saves points down there, and it's tougher for the bad guys to move; they've got hills and forests to get around, and it's good ambush country for us. What we would really like to see is a situation where they have outrun some of their larger threat systems, such as the SA-8, and get them down to the point where all they've got is ZSUs along with SA-7s. Even that would be a pretty good threat to work. We might be able to pick out some of those fellers, or get them into a state where they have a limited reload capability for a given time, or maybe catch an advance party. It all depends on the scenario.

'I have talked to the commanders that have been attached to us, and I have a feeling that they will primarily use us for close air support. But if they get to a situation where they have a high value target that they don't have any other assets for, we may get tasked to go deeper. Some people envision an invasion coming through Central Europe being, from an air defence viewpoint, as being uniform across the whole length of Germany. I don't think it's going to be like that. Even up in the north, where the Warsaw Pact forces will have better radar coverage because the terrain is flatter, there will be some places where the cover is thick, and others where it is thin. Hopefully the intelligence community will retain the initiative, and they will gain a good idea of the battlefield defences, so that if we are tasked to go deep, intelligence can tell us where the seams are; we can penetrate those and head for the target. Once we get through the initial FLOT, I think we can start wandering around deep into West Germany until we get to the high value defences of whatever the target is. A lot of people talk in terms of how far behind the enemy lines we want to go. As far as I am concerned, if you are going up against a motorised rifle division or whatever, straight down their teeth, two feet over is as bad as two clicks [kilometres] is as bad as 20 clicks, whereas if we could determine where the seams are in this particular frontal area and had the fuel and the latitude to go around through the seams, then I think we could go 25, 30, even 50 miles deep. We've got a baseball term which says "hit 'em where they ain't". If we can find those holes, we've got a much better chance of being survivable there, although once we hit the point defences at the target, we're not quite so well off as some of

Right:
For 'Red Flag' exercises a data link pod is carried, usually blue in colour. It can be seen here inboard of the ECM pod. *Frank Mormillo*

Below:
Inboard leading-edge slats extended and carrying two Mavericks, a JAWS Warthog reefs around just a few feet above the terrain. An ALQ-131 ECM pod can be seen beneath the port wing. *Fairchild*

the fast movers, because their speed advantage reduces the time that they are in the threat envelope. But going slower allows you to see more of what is going on.

'The two-ship is the basic element. We like to work a two-ship approach although it may be four, it may be six, or whatever. The types of formation we fly are not all that tough to do; the ground is 300ft away and your wingman is a couple of thousand feet away. I am generally going to have my wingman fly his airplane in a position without a lot of respect to mine, but I want to be able to see him so that I can cover him against both the air and the missile threat. Co-ordinated two-ships is the term we use; we may travel out in a chain of six or eight, modified to suit the circumstances. It helps to fly the leader at a higher altitude than the rest, it's easier for him to navigate, and it highlights him so that the rest of the guys behind don't have to spend a lot of time on checking where he is, so they can look around.

'We don't really want to know about a tank on a treeline; we would rather be given a target area. The senior flight lead organises the attack; he can sector the area either geographically or by time, and decide whether he wants to sequence people in or all go in at once. There are options, decoying the defences for example. If he can determine the edge of the threat envelope and is leading a six-ship attack, he could have his centre two-ship pull up at the edge of the envelope to draw the fire, then go back down again, while the other guys go in and hit it. There is a lot of variety. He can use a sort of line attack or a trail attack, or perhaps have one element use the gun and another fire Maverick.

'Recognition is always a problem. It has to be visual, and the visibility conditions out there [West Germany] are not good. A lot depends on Intelligence. The more we know about the battlefield, the less we have got to find out. If you are lucky enough to have a situation where you know that there are no friendlies in the area it simplifies the problems a lot; we can be much more effective with no constraints. We would like to concentrate on the Warpac counter-air systems first, but it is terribly difficult to distinguish between a T-72 and one of their heavy field guns,

or even a ZSU-23/4 unless he's shooting at you There is going to be a hell of a learning curve ou there on the first day of a war.

'We use the Pave Penny pod a lot to identify targets. It's an excellent system for picking ou specific targets, right down to an individual truck or tank. The Brits are right now the best users o the designator; if a laser spot is put on a target, i shows up on our HUD. You can pick it out o treelines or whatever. The disadvantage is that the people on the ground using the designator give their position away when they designate a target

's like turning on a light at night; they don't want to be sitting out there with the designator on for long. Of course, we may not want to lase the target directly. [Note: It is only necessary if laser-guided weapons are carried.] What we may want done is for the friendly position to be designated, so that everything past that has to be bad guys; this gives us a free fire zone ahead of the laser marked area. We've inadvertently tried that out here; in a training exercise a couple of trainee backs put the laser on our own positions. Luckily nothing developed out of it, but the potential for disaster

Left:
The first European tests of the IIR Maverick were carried out from Ramstein in 1978. An example can be seen under the port wing of the lead aircraft, which is followed by a JAWS 'Afrika Korps revisited' painted machine.
Hughes Missile Division

Above:
Light blotches on a dark ground were also tried during the JAWS evaluation. *Fairchild*

was always there. If we use laser designation for either target or troop recognition, we have to be very careful that everybody knows what we are doing. The trouble is that we think that communications are going to be difficult to work. We try to get things down to where communications are limited, but we still go for visual recognition above all.

'What I think you are going to see on a modern battlefield is different to before. Most people think of support as a flight going in with outriggers, but because of the communications problems and all the other rigmarole, both in the air and because we will be working from dispersed bases, we have evolved a concept where support is given in specific areas of both space and time. We arrive at the right place at the right time, do our thing for the right length of time, then go. We don't necessarily need to co-ordinate with the rest of the world that's going in there. Let me explain how we would do that. The rules we work to are that the choppers have got treetop level and below, and in peacetime we are talking about 100ft above that. If the shooting starts, I think we would be down to the treetops too, especially up north where there is very little terrain to hide behind. 100ft is the lowest we go. It causes all sorts of problems at that level. As long as we are over friendly territory we will drive to and from the target area at between 300 and 500ft. Coming lower makes navigation a little more difficult because your perspective changes. Things that were mere vertical developments from

300ft become towers at low level. Some things, like radio towers, don't change as you come down, they are much the same whether you are at 250ft or driving your car. Other things that you may be able to see and key on, such as being able to recognise a group of buildings as a town, is not so easy. We train a lot in the actual operational areas; and once familiar with them so we can pick out a hill or a prominent lake. As far as I am concerned all altitude training just disappears; that's the point where, if you need to, you will be able to work at 100ft, and you may even be able to hide behind a house; even a bungalow may become a player for you. Apart from navigation, the workload is higher down low. You are looking at a hell of a lot more power lines that you didn't have to worry about higher up, and that makes it a little tough. But you are going to have to expose yourself at some point to hostile fire, trees, telephone poles and what else. You don't get a free war; you don't get to shoot at guys who don't shoot back. We figure on staying around for longer than one pass. Our concept is to stay over, if not friendly territory, then at least neutral areas, from an air defence standpoint, working the target area from between 15 minutes and half an hour.

'Maverick is our main weapon, it gives us a good stand-off capability, and the more we can stand-off, the better we like it. It also gives us a higher P_k than the gun. The electro-optical Maverick works on contrast, dark against light or light against dark. Sure they can camouflage their

Above:
Two 354th TFW aircraft taxi out for a 'Red Flag' mission from Indian Springs auxiliary field. *Frank Mormillo*

anks to reduce the contrast, but they can't do it or all situations. Unless the fighting is in the winter, the camouflage will be a combination of dark colours, which is fine among the trees, but when they move into open fields, then they will have the contrast. If they go to lighter colours, they will stand out in the treelines. To use the EO [electro-optical] Maverick you have to roll in; to et the gross angle you have to point the airplane t the target. You get the dive angle from the way t's set up. You do the gross aiming with the HUD, s soon as you get the pipper on the target you ave to come back inside to your TV screen and ne tune the aiming cross with a control on the hrottle, and lock the missile on. The younger guys who play a lot of video games become very good at , they can do it in two seconds if the original oresight on the HUD was good enough. Some of s older guys take a bit longer. The aiming cross an be space-stabilised so that the pitch of the airplane does not affect it. Generally we know where the selected Maverick is looking because it s based on the HUD setting. Once we launch, we et back close to the ground and head back to the P.

'We have recently got the IR Maverick, which has a better ability through smoke and haze than the TV version. It also increases our stand-off range, and I think it's going to be a very effective tool. It is also easier to lock up. With the IR Maverick we can actually programme where the boresight looks to within, say, x amount of mils on the sight. We can lock the missile on to a target and inform it that that is where you want the boresight to be. It will stay there for however long you want it, even through repeated cycles of the electrical system, so that when you fly the jet on the next mission, it is still boresighted for what you did on the previous one. It gives more flexibility, because you can drive the boresight down so that you can be driving along level and still have the pipper where you want it. You need less dive angle using the IR Maverick, and sometimes no dive angle at all.

'I think that with the visibility that we get in this particular theatre of operations, we could use a weapon for intermediate ranges, between where we use the gun and where we use the Maverick. Something like a point and shoot rocket, where all we need to do is pull to the outside, point and shoot, with a reasonable P_k. The range needs to be between 1½ and 2 miles. [See Hypervelocity Missile, Chapter 4.]

'That big gun is a super weapon, and aiming it is simple. It is effective against ZSU-23/4s and soft vehicles at ranges of between one and two miles. We have a gun-aiming cross on the HUD, and that stays on all the time. We just put the cross on the target and pull the trigger; there may be some small corrections for cross-winds and so forth, but the shells are very heavy and the aim is very true, and down at 2,000ft slant range, if we don't destroy a tank, we are going to get enough hits to stand a good chance of knocking a tread off, or jamming the turret. A few years ago, back in the USA, we were exercising with the Army, using practice rounds. One of the Army tanks got a little bit ahead of the scenario and got himself in with the target array. An A-10A was coming in hot, cleared to fire, and he knocked a tread off and jammed the turret, and that was just with ball ammunition! Luckily no-one got hurt, but it sure rang the chimes real good!'

Finally, Lt-Col Burke sums up his feelings on the A-10A in a war scenario.

'I think that if we can get the first couple of guys in the first wave stopped, this will force the rest of the column, or attack echelon, or whatever they are using, to start manoeuvring around, causing confusion, then we'll really be able to get at 'em. If the terrain is restrictive, we'll get them stopped, and if not, we'll sure slow them down.'

6   Flying the Bird

No-one would ever call the Warthog pretty, and compared to most sleek modern jets, the kindest comment is that it lacks glamour. Its appearance reflects in its performance. It is unable to blast off the runway into a vertical climb, a trick that even the elderly Phantom can perform, and it has no Warp Factor 10 capability to add a certain cachet. Under these circumstances, one could be forgiven for thinking that the A-10A is a real elderly aunt of an aircraft, to be shunned like the plague by the self-assured steely-eyed fast jet drivers and regarded as only slightly more exciting to fly than a Herkybird. Appearances are deceptive; while the Warthog has 'user-friendly' handling character- istics, its low-level, high rate of turn manoeuvre capability and roll response make for an exciting ride — so much so that a considerable proportion of pilots who fly it made it their first choice when they finished pilot training.

In July 1976, *Air Force Magazine* published an interview with four highly experienced pilots from the A-10A Joint Test Force. All were unanimous in praising the aircraft; various handling points that emerged were the comfortable cockpit with its excellent view, simple instrumentation and high set stick position; the remarkable way in which the A-10A could be spun around in a small area; the first class harmonisation of the controls; and the fact that the machine was viceless. Spinning was almost unknown; pro-spin control settings had to be held for between 10 and 15 seconds before the spin would start; while to recover, the controls were returned to the neutral position and the aircraft would return to controlled flight immedi- ately. Vertical stalls had been tried and were described as 'kinda fun', which is hardly the case with the average fast jet.

Stalling at low altitude was felt to be no problem; a slight easing of back pressure on the stick recovered the bird easily enough, although at A-10A operational altitudes there would be little room for error. A stick shaker was fitted to warn the pilot that he was straying into the area of lost control. The ease of flying allowed the pilot to get on with the main job, which was navigating at low level across country, and finding and hitting the target. Roll response was high, even with a heavy bombload beneath the wings, although naturally a little performance was lost. Simulated defensive breaks had been practised, which took the aircraft from 1,000ft down to 50ft with wings level in 7

seconds flat, a feat beyond the capability of most fast jets, involving as it does a steep dive followed by a hard low level pull-out. Low altitude loops were an A-10A speciality at air displays, although this was done once too often at Le Bourget in the late 1970s, resulting in the loss of both aircraft and pilot. This in fact highlighted a weakness; the austere avionics fit did not include a ground collision avoidance warning system.

The austere avionics also meant that, to be truly effective, the Warthog drivers had to be able to map-read their way across country, and ideally also had to be familiar with their designated operating area, although an inertial navigation system was added at a later date. This led Brig-Gen Rudolph F. Wacker, the first com- mander of the Bentwaters A-10A Wing, to comment in 1980 that his pilots needed calibrated eyeballs. Some pilots converting from afterburning types had difficulty in getting used to the lack of instant extra thrust on demand, but they soon learned to plan ahead to keep their energy levels up, while all were impressed by its responsiveness in all three axes; even when fully stalled it retained roll control, while lateral control was retained at any but the slowest speeds.

Of course, no aircraft is totally without foibles, as one young Warthog driver found in 1983. After carrying out a low angle gun pass, he pulled out at 500ft, when suddenly the A-10A's nose pitched down, giving zero g, while at the same time yawing violently. His instant reaction was to haul back on the stick while checking the instruments. Most of the caution lights were on, and the engines

appeared to be winding down as though they had flamed out. The options appeared to be limited to either engine relight or ejection, and with one hand on the bang seat handle, he retarded the throttles. As he did so, he noticed a loss of thrust, which meant that the engines were still operating, so he at once firewalled the throttles and levelled out. What had happened was a massive electrical failure that had tripped off the generators, causing the instruments to wind down, while the pitch-down and yaw was due to the stability augmentation system going out. The final clue was provided by the engine core rev counters which operate independently of the main power source

Above:
'Red Flag 84-4', and a 355th TTW aircraft heads for the range carrying two oddly shaped and unidentifiable pods, possibly ECM. *Frank Mormillo*

Left:
The Warthog has a remarkably fine accident record, but this aircraft is an exception. Pictured landing at RAF Mildenhall on 29 May 1977, it failed to complete a low altitude loop at the Paris Air Show just five days later. The 97 on the engine pod is the Paris Air Show number.
P. A. Rowlings

and which were still functioning. The distraction caused by a panel full of warning lights and an unexpected movement in both vertical and lateral planes had caused the pilot to overlook the fact that the engines were both functioning correctly. His level out took place at a safe 5,000ft, and he recovered to base with little difficulty. The moral of this story is that no military aircraft, no matter how docile its handling, is ever totally trouble-free, and the A-10A, despite its simplicity, is no exception.

So far we have recorded the reactions of experienced pilots to the Warthog. For the other side of the coin, let us listen to the impressions of a young first-tour A-10A pilot.

Capt Mike Ryan is a native of Pennsylvania. His father flew B-17s and A-26s, so an interest in flying was there from an early age. He entered the Air Force Academy at Colorado Springs and, after graduating, went to pilot training on T-37s and T-38s. On completing the course he applied to join an A-10A unit. The A-10A pilots spend more time than most in the air, and this was one of the prime considerations behind his choice; Warthog drivers stack up fighter hours comparatively quickly. After the conversion course at Davis-Monthan AFB, in Arizona, his first operational posting was to the 509th TFS, one of the six squadrons which make

Above:
Capt Mike Ryan, first tourist and flight commander with the 81st TFW, 509th TFS at RAF Bentwaters, seen here as a lieutenant during his Warthog conversion course at Davis-Monthan AFB, Arizona. *Mike Ryan*

Below:
Capt Mike Ryan's certificate for firing the GAU-8/A for the first time.

Be it known to all men present, that
2Lt Michael C. Ryan
"did it in the bathtub" for the first time on 9 Sep 83 A.D.
and proved, once again, that A-10 pilots have a bigger gun.
attest Michael Brown Lt Col

Above:
Some idea of the size of the Thunderbolt II can be gauged from this picture of the A-10A demonstration team, based at Davis Monthan AFB, with the assigned aircraft. The groundcrew are on the wing, and two pilots, Capt Richard B. Betz (left) and Capt James L. Kelley Jr (right), carry out the flying and narration during the demonstration.

Left:
Despite its size and ungainly appearance, the Warthog is extremely agile, as this wingover demonstrates. *RAF*

up the 81st TFW at Bentwaters/Woodbridge. By late 1986 he had amassed about 900 hours on type and, most exceptionally for a first tourist, had become both an instructor pilot and a flight commander.

'To start with at Davis-Monthan, they take you out to show you the aircraft, and also the gun. The gun is very impressive, but the immediate thing about the A-10A is how big it is. The training airplanes we have in the United States are quite small; for instance you can stand on the ground beside a T-37 and look down into the cockpit, but the A-10A is really a monstrous thing; you have to climb a ladder to get into it.

Left:
The 917th TFG based at Barksdale take their Warthogs very seriously. The white 'lazy H' outlined in black is an aim point for the flight refuelling boom operator. The push-in panel over the receptacle shows signs of much usage, and it is interesting that a small black anti-glare panel is retained.

Right:
A factory-fresh A-10A of the 57th TTW takes on fuel over the Nevada desert near Las Vegas. *Fairchild*

Inset:
Not much detail of the aircraft is visible, but this is an excellent 'tanker's-eye view' shot of the Warthog in action. *Mike Ryan*

'The conversion course is in phases. First you get seven rides, and that teaches you just to fly the airplane. You fly circuits, you fly overhead patterns and things like that, and find out what its limits are. The first time you sit in it, you look out over the wings and you look down over the back of the airplane, and the sheer size of it gives you a great feeling of being alone. That's a tremendous feeling; you are the one who is going to have to handle it. That is the way that real pilots like to feel. The first time that I got to fly the A-10A, we started up and taxied out, then there was an emergency that closed the runway for an hour, so we just had to sit there. I sat there in that great airplane all by myself for an hour, which was great. I got to relax and think about what I was doing. Normally when you fly a training mission you are always too busy for that, and you don't realise what you have done until after you get back.'

There is no two-seat conversion trainer for the A-10A, and the usual procedure during the course is for an instructor to fly a chase aircraft, instructing the pupil by radio.

'The first day I went out, the instructor in the chase plane — and that is something totally different to having an instructor on board — said "turn in front of that cloud over there". Now the airplane we fly before the A-10A is the T-38, which is supersonic. It takes about three counties to turn around in because it is so fast. There was a huge wall of cloud off to one side, and I thought that if I turned, I'd go right into it. Did I get a surprise. When you do a turn in the A-10A, it's virtually turning inside itself. You just put a wingtip on the ground (not literally), haul back on the stick, and the airplane just turns right around it.

'Other first things I remember, everybody tells you that when you come in to land, don't try to flare; just fly the airplane straight into the runway. Now it's a straight-winged airplane, and it flies a lot like the T-37, but you don't land it like a T-37. For a start, you are about 25ft higher in the air than in a T-37, and it's a much heavier machine.

'The instrument setup is like that of the T-38, so the transition is relatively quick. Also, being we were in Arizona, we never flew in the weather so we didn't have that added to the workload. At the end of the first seven rides, the guys are not only ready to move on, they are anxious to do so. Compared to the T-38, the Warthog is heavy on the controls, but for the size of the airplane, it rolls very smartly. Just to sit in it, you would think it

would be like flying a B-17, but it's not, it's so responsive. And the way it turns . . . when we prepare our low level maps, we do it a lot differently to the fast movers. The F-4s and such, they have these big turning arcs that they have to draw on the map. We don't do that; this airplane turns so well that we just draw the angle. We square the corners; this airplane flies square corners very well. Later in the course, we start to do air combat. We have to follow the instructor, and he'll put a very sharp turn on you. You'll look at it and think "there's no way I'm going to make this turn", because you are used to flying a T-38. You just think, well, I'll pull as hard as I can, and the result is you make the turn right there.

'After the initial seven rides, we went to the bombing range. The A-10A is such a stable bombing platform that the guys caught on quick and generally got good scores. We also fired the gun for the first time. That is something everybody wonders about before they do it. You've heard about the pipper on the gunsight being called the death dot? Well that's just what it is. You put the pipper on the target, pull the trigger, and the target just dies. Although we don't have a windage computer for aiming the gun, the shells come out so fast that the target just explodes. Of course, the first time you fire the gun, it's for a score on a controlled range. It's not like fighting a tank out in the desert. You pull the trigger, there's a vibration, smoke from the gun goes over the canopy, and that's it. And because none of us had fired another gun, we had nothing to compare it with.'

After discussing the A-10A conversion course, Capt Ryan went on to talk about operational aspects of the ordinary pilot at squadron level.

'In the early days of the Warthog, all you heard about was how accurate the gun was, and how easy it was to use. This may have been because the guys flying it were all very experienced, I don't know, but in fact we have had a few problems, although they are all fairly minor. The greatest problem that new guys have is doing what we call track-shoot-track, where you track the target, you shoot, and then you continue to track after you've left off firing. When they first put the gun in the airplane and fired it, it caused the nose to pitch up. They compensated for that, but then the high spin rate of the great heavy rotor forces the nose down, so they fixed the SAS [stability augmentation system] to compensate through the elevator. Now they are having to rework the compensation. The guns on the airplane are now at the point where they all react differently. On some airplanes the nose will tuck under quite considerably, while on others it won't. We are getting it licked, but at the moment we have a board on our squadron where we write down how all the guns react. It is still a very accurate weapon, and we could if necessary fire a three- to four-second burst, but we need to know what is going to happen when we press the trigger. Basically though, we don't employ it that way; we fire a one-second burst, then move to a different target and fire another one-second burst.

Another problem we had when firing the gun, a lot of smoke and residue comes back over the canopy and sticks to it. It was difficult coming off the range into the sun; you couldn't see a lot. There's a Winchel wash system for the windshield, but that just smears everything around. How we are getting over that now, we are fitting a gun gas diverter to the nose which forces the gun gases out into the airflow. The diverter also takes out the apparent vibration. I say apparent vibration, because when you shoot the gun, the airplane doesn't vibrate, but it seems like it, and if you look at the camera film it also seems that the airplane is vibrating, and it makes it hard to track. The thing that give this impression is the gun gas turbulence as it flows past the canopy. Now with the diverter, all the gas goes underneath, and so the airplane doesn't appear to move, and the gun cross doesn't seem to vibrate. It was just an illusion. In fact, with the diverter fitted the gun even sounds quieter.

'Maverick is a super weapon, and the new IR Maverick is even easier to use. The way we do it, we know where the Maverick is looking through the HUD, and we put the dot on the target with Maverick full up [activated]. Then we look down to the TV screen, and if we did it properly, the target is right there in front of the aiming cross. That's how good you can get on Maverick. There wasn't ever a problem for me, and the only problem for new guys comes if they don't actually get it aligned the first time, and they try to realign. We teach new guys, if you don't get it the first time, or very shortly after, break off, don't try to transition too much. [If too long is spent in aiming, the A-10A become vulnerable to the ground defences, which are given enough time to acquire, predict, track and fire.]'

In addition to hostile surface-to-air defences, the A-10A must be prepared to defend itself against enemy fighters. In terms of basic performance figures it appears to be a turkey in the dogfight; it is large and angular, and this makes it easier to see in close combat, giving an advantage to smaller, sleeker adversaries. But appearances can be deceptive. Many of the advantages of the dedicated air combat fighter are lost down in the weeds where the Warthog habitually operates; turning capability is a function of speed and the A-10A will always be able to out-turn a faster opponent, and generally force it to overshoot, at which point the hunter becomes the hunted. If an air superiority fighter was unwise enough to slow down to tackle an A-10A, it would still find that it could be out-turned in most cases. At typical

94

Warthog speeds, even the F-16 cannot turn with it, although much will depend on pilot skill and ability. Capt Ryan discusses air combat, having first made the point that the primary role of the A-10A is close air support, and that air combat will only be undertaken by pilots if it is forced on them.

'We have a very involved air-to-air training programme for self-defence, so that we can survive en route to the battlefield. We are the slowest guys in town, so we end up looking over our shoulders a lot. In wartime, in an area where there was not much of an air threat, we would fly to and from the battle area at a comfortable altitude, say between 250 and 500ft. Our guys get very comfortable at those sort of heights. When the threat dictated, we would go down to 100ft, although the workload is high down there, and it can be very fatiguing. At that level, the air threat is not a factor. [Not even look-down, shoot-down missiles are very good against such low level targets.] If a bad guy wants to skyline us to use a missile, he has to come down to 50ft, and by all means let him. Down there he's got all sorts of problems that we're not concerned with. If he tries to gun us, he is either going to overshoot or stall. I think we'd see him first, we check six quite a bit, and being centred on the North German plain, we think that we're the best in the business. I don't say that lightly; during one of our recent exercises we had F-15s and F-16s tasked against our squadron for four days straight, and they didn't get a lot of kills. We got six belly kills on them as they overshot, and that was with the gun.'

At the time of writing, in late 1986, trials were afoot to give the A-10A a credible defensive capability by equipping them with up to four AIM-9L Sidewinders to supplement the gun, which is a comparatively short ranged weapon, while its sighting system is not optimised for air combat.

'I think giving us Limas [Sidewinders] is a fantastic idea. We're not out here to be aces; we're out here to win the ground battle, but with our turn radius, any threat aircraft has to honour the fact that we have a Lima, and that it gives us a threat range beyond that of our gun, and that we're going to shoot it in his face. This means that the bad guys are not going to want to play with us.

'I was once a mission commander on a "Red Flag" package, and from that experience I can say that the A-10s from Bentwaters are the best in self-defence. We've yet to fall pregnant in any exercise that I've been on. The thing we like about the Warthog is its single seat; we do our own thing, and there's nobody in the world that knows what flying an A-10A is like except an A-10A pilot. We take great pride in it.'

Below:
Death dot: 'You put the pipper on the target, pull the trigger, and the target just dies.' Here a captured Soviet T-62 MBT is destroyed by the GAU-8/A. *Fairchild*

7 What Might Have Been

There are several odd features in the history of the A-10A Thunderbolt II. The first, and operationally least important, is the name. It was called after a previous Republic fighter, the P-47 Thunderbolt, which, although designed as an air superiority fighter, gained an enviable reputation in the attack role during the closing years of World War 2. Early jet fighters from Republic (not yet taken over by Fairchild) also used names beginning with Thunder, from the F-84 Thunderjet of 1946 vintage, through the swept-winged derivatives which were the F-84F Thunderstreak and the RF-84F Thunderflash, through the revolutionary XF-91 Thunderceptor with its inverse taper wing, to the Mach 2 capable F-105 Thunderchief which gave such sterling service in the skies of North Vietnam. At this stage, names beginning with Thunder were in distinctly short supply, although Thundercloud and Thunderstorm were possibles, but Thunderbox was definitely unsuitable. It was perhaps inevitable that the name of Thunderbolt would be revived for the new attack aircraft, even though a few P-47s were still around in the service of South American countries. The decision was long delayed, and not until the 100th A-10A was handed over to the USAF at Hagerstown on 3 April 1978 did 'Thunderbolt II' become official. Red decals were stuck on the nose of the aircraft for the ceremony, which was attended by two P-47 aces: Brig-Gen 'Gabby' Gabreski, and Col Robert S. Johnson. A few hours later the decals were removed, which in a way was prophetic. The name 'Warthog' proposed by Maj Major some five years earlier had already stuck. During the preparation of this book the writer came into contact with many people closely associated with the A-10A, and it has been very noticeable that not one of them, whether service or manufacturer, ever referred to the aircraft by its correct name.

Neither has it had any success on the export market, although several countries have evaluated it. This is rather surprising when one considers that by modern standards it is cheap, both to acquire and to operate, and is simple both to fly and to maintain. Its reputation as a dedicated tank-buster hardly helped, although it is in fact capable of carrying out almost all missions bar interception and troop-carrying. A Fairchild brochure issued in 1980 lists a round dozen missions that the A-10A is capable of carrying out: they are close air support, interdiction, medium to high altitude bombing, counter-insurgency, forward air control, armed reconnaissance, anti-helicopter, landing zone preparation, convoy (the land type) escort, combat rescue, forward deployment, and maritime defence. It would therefore seem to be ideal for many smaller nations, and especially those with an insurgency problem or a fractious neighbour. Of course, politics enters into the picture here: even in the USA, many people still cannot grasp the concept of a slow jet, and what it can do that a fast jet cannot. In a nutshell, the Warthog lacks glamour, and in the export market capability cannot compete with the spurious cachet of a supersonic fighter. Another political handicap was the depleted uranium gun ammunition, which tends to be sensitive. While we have seen earlier that of itself U238 is pretty harmless stuff, the use of it is a propaganda weapon for those on the receiving end. 'Radioactive bullets used' would make a great headline, and of course it can hardly be denied that the stuff is radioactive. Any attempt to state the true level of radioactivity would look like a whitewash.

Another politically sensitive point is that U238 can be processed into the highly lethal plutonium, although this demands a full-scale nuclear reactor, and countries that own these would hardly need to bother about pinching the DU core from the projectiles of the GAU-8/A. Oddly enough, this is not considered sufficient reason to prevent U238 from being used as balance weights for the control surfaces in many civil airliners, or to restrict sales of the said airliners to certain countries. Viewed objectively, the whole question of restricting the sales of DU shells to certain countries seems a bit of a nonsense, and it would be certain to hinder sales of the A-10A. It is understandable that any nation paying out for an aircraft that had been designed around a very special gun would want the special ammunition to go with it.

Countries showing interest were Morocco, the United Arab Emirates and Korea, to all of whom a strong sales pitch was made. Egypt and Turkey were also possible candidates, while Australia was offered a two-seat night-capable version, of which more later. The British Labour Government was reported to have shown an interest in 1978, although there is no evidence that the RAF had a requirement for a dedicated tank-buster, and this raised Fairchild's hopes of a deal involving Great

Britain, West Germany and Italy for a variant powered by an unaugmented version of the TurboUnion RB199 as used on Tornado. But at the end of the day, all came to naught.

The final odd feature of the A-10A is that while it has been built in large numbers, it has barely changed at all. The first pre-production machine was an A-10A, while the 705th and final production aircraft was also an A-10A, which was accepted by the USAF on 20 March 1984. Counting the two YA-10 development prototypes and the six pre-production machines, the final total was 713, just 20 short of the original requirement of 733. Various extras have been nailed on to the operational aircraft from time to time, such as the INS, the Pave Penny pod and other avionics items, while the ACES II ejector seat has supplanted the original Escapac, but the changes have never been radical enough to warrant a change from the A suffix.

There were a variety of reasons for this, but all of them stemmed from lack of money. A defence budget has to be shared among all the services, and is theoretically allocated according to need. In practice there is never enough to go round, and each service has to make do with what it can get. Closely contemporary with the A-X programme was that for the F-X air superiority fighter, which materialised as the F-15 Eagle. The Eagle was very large, tremendously capable and colossally expensive, and it soon became clear that the Air Force was not going to be able to afford as many as it would have liked. As a result, a further programme was instituted for a lightweight austere fighter which could supplement the F-15 in the air superiority role, and also carry a worthwhile load of air-to-ground weapons. This duly became the F-16 Fighting Falcon, which was unofficially dubbed the 'swing fighter' because of its ability to switch roles at need.

The result was predictable. The F-15, F-16 and A-10A were all competing for the available funds, and there were many who wanted the CAS mission to be carried out by the F-16, which would have meant junking the A-10A altogether. Fortunately this did not happen, but it did effectively prevent all but relatively minor upgrades to the angular but effective tank-buster; and it almost certainly

Below:
The large size of the A-10A is highlighted by the adjacent MiG-15UTI, F-16 and MiG-21 in this oddball USAF/ Egyptian Air Force formation. *USAF*

caused further production, and development of a two-seat version, to be curtailed.

Of the many proposals that Fairchild made down the years, the two that came nearest to fruition were both two-seaters: a conversion trainer, and a dedicated night and all-weather variant.

It had always been customary for the Air Force Reserve (AFRes) and the Air National Guard (ANG) to receive Air Force cast-offs. In the case of the A-10A it was decided to equip certain AFRes and ANG units with new-build machines. While the Warthog is reckoned to be so easy to fly that regular Air Force pilots do not need a dual control trainer to help them convert, it was considered that AFRes and ANG pilots were not quite in the same category, and a total of 30 dual control aircraft, provisionally designated A-10Bs, were ordered in 1980. The A-10B was soon cancelled on financial grounds, and experience has proved this to be a correct decision; the part-time flyers have proved to be perfectly up to the task of converting on a single-seater. The night and all-weather attack version was a rather more complex and protracted story.

War does not cease at sunset. The Soviet Union knows this very well and has for many years practised night manoeuvres with its armoured divisions. During the last few years it has also extended this capability to its battlefield helicopter units. Air power is by contrast more limited, and with the exception of a few units of very specialised, and very expensive, aircraft, is almost helpless at night — although, to be fair, many counter-air systems that rely on electro-optical

target acquisition and guidance are not a lot of use either. Weather is yet another factor. In clear skies, in summer in southern latitudes, darkness descends for only about six hours during the 24. At the other extreme, in northern Norway in winter, even in clear skies, darkness is almost total; while in the most likely anticipated area of conflict, Central Europe, the weather in winter, if it does not stop flying altogether, puts severe restrictions on the types of operations that can be flown without special equipment. Something like three hours in the 24 during the month of January is par for the course, while even summer does not lack for adverse weather, with low cloud and haze restricting visibility. While the A-10A was designed to be able to operate beneath much of the weather, the case for extending its capabilities to include the hours of darkness and worse weather conditions was unarguable.

This need had been foreseen at the time when
the A-X specification had been drafted. One of the
requirements was that it had to be able to be
modified into a two-seater with the back seat
carrying a Weapons Systems Officer (WSO —
commonly pronounced Whizzo). The first pre-
production aircraft was bailed back from the Air
Force, and modifications began in April 1978.
Having been used extensively in the Air Force Test
& Evaluation programme, this aircraft already
carried extensive flight test instrumentation, which
saved both time and expense. It was officially
designated the YA-10B, but it was almost
universally referred to as the N/AW A-10.

Converting the A-10A into a two-holer was
quite an easy task. The second seat was to be
mounted above the ammunition drum, with the
back-seater's eye level some 10in higher than that
of the pilot, allowing the WSO to look over the top
of the pilot's helmet, and giving him almost the
same angle of view over the nose. To do this, the
structure behind the front cockpit was removed,
and the decking above the ammunition drum was
strengthened to form the cockpit floor. The
titanium bathtub could not realistically be
extended — nor does it seem that it was ever
intended to be, not even on the production article
— but a thin layer of titanium armour was spaced
just beneath the aluminium skin to the sides, with
the additional layer of nylon spalling protection. A
sloping bulkhead with seat support rails was
added, plus a canopy support bow in the
intermediate position. Both canopies opened
sideways to the right, an arrangement that had
been suggested for the single-seat A-10A, but
rejected. The avionics black boxes displaced by the
second seats were relocated in the space beneath
the fairing needed to streamline the double canopy
back to the original lines of the fuselage. The only
other structural change was to the fins, which were
heightened by roughly 20in to compensate for the
potentially destabilising effect of the increased
depth of the forward fuselage along the line of the
twin cockpits. In total, the structure weight
increased by a mere 521lb.

The rear crew position contained flying controls
and many of the instruments necessary for flight,
arranged in the same layout as in the front
position. Two small CRTs were installed, the
upper being for the FLIR/LLTV and the lower for
the radar display and the Maverick TV picture.
Various other instruments and controls filled the
side consoles. The control column in the rear
position was about 4in shorter than standard.

The front cockpit changed little. A few
instruments were rearranged to make room for a
modern Kaiser HUD, and both crew were seated
on ACES II ejection seats. A second environ-
mental control system was added; neither the
A-10A nor the N/AW A-10 had any provision for
pressurisation.

The essence of an aircraft able to carry out the
close air support mission at night or in adverse
weather conditions is that it must be liberally
equipped with sensors. The short nose with its
huge gun was unsuitable for carrying a radar, and
this was mounted in a pod beneath the port wing.
The radar was a modified Westinghouse WX-50
weather radar, with ground mapping, moving
target indicator, terrain avoidance and terrain
following modes. It was quite a small thing, and
was controlled from the rear seat. The scan width
was ±30° in azimuth, and it had selectable range
scales of 5nm, 10nm or 15nm. It also showed the
ground contours ahead at distances of 1nm and
2nm which were projected on the pilot's HUD. It
was not an automatic terrain-following system; it
had to be flown manually. Simple and short-
ranged, it was also very reliable.

Radar back-up was given by the Texas
Instruments AAR-42 FLIR (Forward Looking
Infra-Red) which was carried in a pod beneath the
fuselage. This was also controlled from the rear
cockpit, and while it was normally aligned on the
flightpath with 105mil depression it could be
slewed through ±20° in azimuth and +5° and −35°
in the vertical plane. The FLIR had automatic
contrast enhancement, showing either 'white hot'
or 'dark hot', and had two selectable fields of view;
wide angle, which was 16°×12°, and narrow angle,
which was 4°×3°. In suitable conditions it could be
used for terrain-following flight instead of the
radar, but its main purpose was to identify targets
and permit an accurate attack to be made. The
FLIR imagery could be projected on to the pilot's
HUD at the same time as it was displayed on the
WSO's CRT, but it was normally taken off the
HUD when being slewed off the flight path, as it
could cause the pilot to become disoriented.

Supplemental to the FLIR, and not intended for
use in the production aircraft at first, was the
General Electric Low Light Television (LLTV).
This was carried on the Pave Penny mounting and
had a 30° field of view. Other black boxes carried

were two Honeywell APN-194 radar altimeters, which were invaluable at low altitude at night, a Ferranti Type 105 laser ranger which was boresighted to the FLIR, and a programmable INS, at a time when operational Warthogs did not have such an item. Apart from the obvious, the laser ranger had two other uses. It could be used to accurately measure the distance to significant points to update the INS, and it could be used as a 'walking stick' to assist a let-down in bad conditions if all else failed, giving a continuous update of the slant range to the ground. In fact the performance of both the radar and the FLIR was pretty good, power lines across the Mojave desert being picked up on either at a range of several miles. It should not however be assumed that either would have worked half as well in the cluttered terrain of Central Europe, or the mountains of Korea. Pave Tack, the combined FLIR target acquisition and laser designator pod, was also considered for the trials, but this did not proceed.

Hanging sensor pods all over the N/AW A-10 was done purely to evaluate the system. Had there been a production aircraft, it would have been rather different. For a start, the canopy would have been a single-piece clamshell, opening rearwards, and the windshield would have been a single-piece wrap-around type. The sensors in the pods would have been more permanently housed, freeing the hard-points for weapons. The radar was to have been located in the redesigned front of the left main gear fairing, while the FLIR would have been in a similar position on the other side. The laser ranger was to have been housed in the leading-edge of the starboard wing, and the LLTV, much praised by trials pilots, in the port leading-edge. It was also discovered that the extra height added to the fins was in the main unnecessary; an extra 6in would have been enough.

The additional avionics had caused a weight increase of 1,570lb, although this included the WSO and his ejector seat. Added to the 521lb noted earlier, this increased the clean all-up weight by a total of 2,091lb. This, plus the extra drag, proved to have little effect on performance: the operational radius fell by just 6nm, and the V_{max} by a notional 3kt. Sustained g dropped away slightly, as was only to be expected, but there was little in it.

The modification programme lasted 13 months in all, and the first flight test was made on 4 May 1979. The N/AW A-10 soon proved to handle just like the single-seater, and gun firing trials commenced as early as 23 May. The first four flights were flown in daylight with the pilot under a hood, and the backseater acting as safety pilot, but the next four were flown at night. Three pilots flew

these eight sorties, and averaged 43% hits on a banner target, which at 20ft×20ft was rather bigger than a tank. Target acquisition trials were commenced in August, and the radar demonstrated that it could pick up moving targets at a distance of 7nm. On 1 October the aircraft was handed over to the USAF to conduct its trials; at this point some 65 flights totalling 120 hours had been made.

One of the Fairchild test pilots involved in these trials, commented as follows:

'We flew the whole evaluation in the night attack mode, with a little bit of adverse weather; you don't get much of that at Edwards. Night ground attack has always been the most difficult mission of all. You are operating at low level, at night, against targets that are not discrete; they can move around, you don't know where they are. Staying away from the ground is difficult, that's why we think it needs two people. The pilot is always busy not running into the ground, and the GIB (guy in back, ie WSO) can find the targets and give him some help.

'Firing at night we had no external cues at all, but we still scored 43% on the banner targets. If you hold the sight on for a second after you finish firing, you can see your shots hitting. Later on we went up on a tactical range and hit real targets, tanks, trucks and such. How many hits we got we don't know, but we know we got hits because we could see the sparks. We could see it on the video after.

'Finding the targets could sometimes be a little difficult. We knew roughly where the targets were on the range, so we didn't have to hunt for them much, but what made it difficult was that they had been sitting on the range for years, and were at very low delta temperatures, very low IR contrast. As a result we had to get close to them before we could pick them up on the FLIR. They were slow to heat up in the morning, and quick to cool down at night, so things were different depending on whether we went through before dawn or after sunset, or in the middle of the night. Sometimes the tank would be cooler than the ground, and sometimes it would be hotter, and that made it real

difficult. The real tanks that we exercised with, had we been able to shoot them, it would have been a piece of cake, they showed up beautifully on the FLIR.

'Using the FLIR, you are only interested in two things, the total temperature and the delta temperature. If you get into the right area, you don't need assistance to tell a tank. The delta temperature is what really shows up. The engine exhaust is actually the lowest heat contrast you can get and some tanks are certainly shielded, so the heat aspects (of the exhaust) are not the best. The best is a combination of the gun barrel, if it's been fired, and the tracks. The tracks generate a lot of heat, and if the ground is very cold, the delta temperature is high, and those hot tank tracks show up clearly.'

USAF trials of the N/AW A-10 commenced on 1 October 1979, and although scheduled to finish in January 1980, lasted until the following March. A few missions were flown with a two-man crew, but rather surprisingly, most of the Air Force evaluation was concerned with single-seat night operation. Fairchild's test pilot gives his views.

'I think it fair to say that we kicked off on that programme with a fair degree of prejudice. The Air Force wanted to do the job single-seat. They were very against a two-seater because they

wanted to have a single-seat solution. The reason they wanted that was because they had so many single-seat airplanes in the inventory: not only A-10As, but A-7s and F-16s, both of which were supposed to be able to do the air-to-ground mission. They very much wanted to have a simple way to go that would make all these single-seat airplanes double up at night. The conclusion that came out was that in certain environments, such as the area they did a lot of the testing in, around Eglin AFB, in Florida, where the terrain is pretty flat, they felt they could do the night attack single-seat, although with some degradation. They still needed all the avionics that we had, radar FLIR and such. The Fairchild concept was to use a two-man crew; we felt that the workload needed two people to do the job. We still believe that.'

Right:
The two-seat Warthog, which first flew in May 1979, is seen in an early test flight from Edwards before the sensors were fitted. *Fairchild*

Below:
How the A-10A could have been developed; a night and adverse weather capable aircraft with a two-man crew, a thinner section wing, revised main gear housing, and much more powerful low bypass ratio engines probably based on the F404. *Fairchild*

The real snag was that a gadget called LANTIRN (Low Altitude Navigation & Targeting by Infra-Red at Night) was under development, which in pod form could be fitted to any combat aircraft to give it a night attack facility, and the USAF was far more interested in acquiring something that would be of advantage across the whole tactical inventory, than yet another specialised type, no matter how capable. Early in 1987, LANTIRN is still not available for fitting to single-seat A-10As, and in fact only 100 are scheduled to receive it.

Various attempts have been made to improve and upgrade the Warthog. Those that have been successful are mainly cheap, and concern the avionics. The Pave Penny laser target finder was adopted from 1978, and the ASN-141 INS was built into the last 283 aircraft from 1980, the rest being scheduled to be retrofitted with completion due in mid-1987. An APN-194 radar altimeter has been incorporated, and the original ALR-46 RWR (Radar Warning Receiver) has been upgraded, first by the ALR-64 and then by ALR-69. Operational aircraft can carry the Westinghouse ALQ-119 ECM pod; better pods are available but the A-10A has less need of them than most. It is not scheduled to receive the ASPJ.

The unsuccessful modifications have either been scrapped or are on back-burner, usually through lack of dollars. The Warthog almost seems to have become a Cinderella among combat aircraft, even if it does look like one of the Ugly Sisters.

Fairchild seems to have become sensitive to criticism about the low speed of the A-10A at a fairly early stage, and for this it can hardly be blamed. A model was exhibited at Farnborough in 1976 with longer and considerably slimmer engine pods, and it was suggested that power could be supplied either by the American YJ-101-GE which had been used to drive the YF-17 prototype, or the European RB-199 under development for Tornado. The extra power and reduced drag (less frontal area for the engine nacelles) would push up the top speed by about 50kt and improve take-off performance and acceleration, but at some cost in endurance and loiter time. There were no takers, but a retrofit scheme followed using General Electric's F404-400D engine, which had been developed from the YJ101 primarily for the F-18. The F404 is one of the most reliable engines ever to enter service, and its use would have pushed up the top speed of the A-10 to 460kt, improved the acceleration and doubled the sustained turn capability from 2.6 to 5.2g at 325kt at sea level. The cost would have been the loss of one hour loiter time on the original designed mission. Improved avionics and night attack capability would meet the mission requirements of the 1990s. The modification for the engines is simple: a new nacelle to be retrofitted. A prototype could be test flown in 1988 and the retrofit programme commenced in 1990.

As stated earlier, pilot workload is high, and the

habitat of the Warthog close to the ground is unforgiving of error. Several aircraft have been lost because the pilot has simply flown into terra firma or an obstruction which he has not evaluated correctly. This in fact was the reason for fitting the radar altimeter. A further proposal has been for a Ground Collision Avoidance Warning System. Developed by Fairchild, and applicable to other aircraft as well as the A-10A, the GCAWS works through three independently operating radar altimeter antennae. The system continuously computes the flight path from bank angle, pitch angle, angle of attack, airspeed, g capability available for manoeuvre, and altitude. The terrain is extrapolated forward in time, and the altitude that will be lost due to pilot response time, roll recovery and dive recovery are added to the terrain clearance limit, and a verbal warning to pull up is given. The warning also sounds when altitude drops below 90ft.

As scheduled production drew to a close, Fairchild made a last desperate effort to secure export orders. Two basic types were promoted, one single-seat night attack, the other a two-seat night attack and combat-ready trainer. The N/AW A-10 was used as the evaluation aircraft for both, and was flown by pilots of the United Arab Emirates during January 1983, a strong sales pitch having been made to the UAE among others.

In an effort to keep costs down, the earlier intention to house the sensors in the airframe was dropped — both radar and FLIR were to be podded and carried on stations four and six respectively, with the laser rangefinder mounted in the FLIR pod, while the LLTV was omitted altogether. A new wide-angle HUD was proposed, with a field of view of 28° in azimuth and 21° in elevation, with a full night raster capability. The instrument panel was to be rearranged to accommodate two multi-function displays on either side of the HUD control panel. These were able to show radar presentations, Maverick and FLIR pictures, operational and armament control data, and a totally new feature, an electronic moving map display, which was not only invaluable for navigation purposes, but showed the aircraft's position and progress in direct relation to the terrain. Optional extras included provision for secure voice communications, anti-jamming and data link, which could all be added to the two Collins AN/ARC-182 VHF radios; while if voice communications beyond line of sight range were required, the AN/ARC-174 radio could be tacked on. Other options were the provision of a mission cassette facility for the INS; and, in podded form, the Pave Penny laser spot seeker or the ATLIS laser designator. Additional weapons options were AIM-9L Sidewinders carried in two pairs on stations 2 and 10 using dual rail launchers, and two

AM-39 Exocet anti-shipping missiles on stations 4 and 8 respectively.

If Exocet seems an odd weapon to propose for an American aircraft, it should be remembered that this was in 1983, and the South Atlantic War was barely a year old. Exocet was news, and it was 'combat proven'. The mystique surrounding it tended to obscure the fact that it had not performed as well as the media made out. To carry it, the A-10A needed compatible ejector-type launchers, and the means of feeding the missile with data on the aircraft velocity and altitude, and the bearing of and distance to the target. AGM-84A Harpoon was another anti-shipping weapon that could be carried.

The two-seat night attack version contained the same sensors and communications kit as the single-seater, but with an extra crewman to share the workload. The rear cockpit contained the major flight and engine instruments, and also flight controls, altough it lacked the HUD. In addition to operations, it could serve as a conventional trainer, although, as we have seen, this was hardly necessary. Roles stressed for this model, in addition to the normal close air support and interdiction, were armed border and coastal patrol and surveillance, an activity for which the Warthog's two-man crew, sensors and long endurance were admirably well suited. Many other types of surveillance and patrol aircraft are unarmed; in an area where opposition might be unexpectedly encountered, not only could it hit back hard, but was better qualified than any other type to survive an initial surprise onslaught.

If the A-10 had been born to controversy, the end of production passed almost unnoticed except by those intimately concerned with it. It promised much, and was capable of considerable development. It could have given sterling service as a multi-role warplane to many air forces around the world. But sadly, none of this came to pass. As one Fairchild man said, very rightly, it just isn't sexy enough!

8 Epilogue

The attitude of the United States Air Force towards the Warthog has always seemed to be a trifle ambivalent. It has done everything that has been asked of it, and has shown considerable development potential. Yet its ability to carry out its designed task has constantly been questioned mainly due to doubts about its ability to survive over a modern battlefield, in spite of the fact that it has performed convincingly against simulated Soviet defences during 'Red Flag' exercises on the Nellis range. The men who fly it exude confidence in spite of the nagging doubts emanating from the high command. The delay in giving the aircraft an official name seems symptomatic of doubts in Air Force minds; an official naming ceremony is more than just putting a handle on to an aircraft to replace a collection of letters and numbers. It is more a rite of acceptance, a form of initiation into the Air Force community, and, like any initiation, delay seems to imply doubts as to the worth of the candidate, and a reluctance to admit him (or, in this case, it). A similar circumstance is currently visible with the B-1B, although it is possible that the reasons there are more to do with the unthinkable nature of its primary mission; the naming of the B-1B would be in a way humanising the inhuman.

The first A-10A unit was designated in November 1974 as being the 355th Tactical Training Wing, based at Davis-Monthan AFB in the Arizona desert. Its first aircraft was delivered on 2 March 1976, and the first A-10A unit to be declared operational was the 33rd Tactical Fighter Training Squadron of the 355th TTW, later that year. Deliveries to operational units began in March 1977, to the 354th TFW based at Myrtle Beach, Florida, this location being chosen because of its proximity to a gunnery range. The 356th TFS, the 'Green Demons', was the first A-10A unit to be declared fully operational in October, and the other squadrons in the wing quickly followed. Meanwhile, A-10As had been received by the 57th TTW based at Nellis AFB in Nevada, whose job it was to develop tactics. Other events were the first deployment to Europe of the type, when it initially appeared at the Farnborough Air Show in September 1976, followed by a tour of USAFE bases; a deployment to Alaska for cold weather trials in January 1977; an extremely successful 'surge' test at Nellis the following month (when the sorties flown passed all expectations and the gun ammunition supply ran out); participation in a 'Red Flag' exercise at Nellis for the first time in April; while the first operational deployment to Europe was carried out by elements of the 355th TTW in August of that year, based at Sembach in West Germany for Exercise 'Valley Forge'. Priority was by this time to permanently deploy A-10A units to Europe.

The original plan was to operate two wings of A-10As in Europe, but this was altered. In February 1978 it ·was announced that the 81st TFW, based at RAF Bentwaters/Woodbridge, two airfields very close together and administratively a single unit, would relinquish its F-4 Phantoms and make way for the Warthog. Instead of two wings in USAFE, the 81st TFW was to be a 'superwing' with six squadrons and 108 aircraft. Bentwaters was to be home, from which the squadrons would deploy to four forward operating locations in Germany.

On 28 June 1978 the wheels started to turn. The 355th TTW, which was the designated A-10A training wing, began Operation 'Ready Thunder', the purpose of which was to convert pilots on to the A-10A for the 81st TFW. Codenames are intended to preserve a measure of security, but 'Ready Thunder' was fooling no-one, and the name was quickly changed to 'Ready Bentwaters'. The first squadron of the new wing was soon converted, and it ferried its aircraft to Bentwaters on 25 January 1979. The 92nd TFS — for it was the unit — was declared mission-ready on arrival, which was stretching it a bit; one does not train for European missions very effectively over the Arizona desert. From this point the 81st TFW became the favoured Warthog unit. As its aircraft fell due for major maintenance, they were ferried back to the USA and exchanged for brand-new aircraft straight from the factory. In this way the 81st TFW retained a constant build standard among its aircraft, and always had the most up-to-date kit. For example, the 81st was the first unit to have INS-equipped Warthogs. This apparent elitism was of course because it faced the greatest threat, and therefore had the greatest need.

The equipment of A-10A units was steady rather than rapid, and the only additional US-based regular Air Force unit to receive the type, other than evaluation units, was the 23rd TFW at England AFB, Louisiana. Deliveries to the Air

National Guard began in April 1979 when the 103rd TFG of the ANG, based at Windsor Locks, Connecticut, received its first aircraft. In all, five ANG units fly the type, which with its ease of operation and maintenance is well suited to the part-timers. This in fact set a precedent; it was the first time that an ANG unit had received new-build aircraft rather than Air Force cast-offs. The Air Force Reserve followed suit in June 1980 when the first A-10A arrived at Barksdale in Louisiana, to commence the equipment of the 917th TFG, the first of five AFRes units to operate the type. Two further USAF units filled out the inventory; the 25th TFS based at Suwon in South Korea from November 1981, and the 18th TFS, which is part of the 343rd Composite Wing, based at Eielson AFB in Alaska, from the following month.

The deployment of the 25th TFS to Suwon is of particular interest. While the war officially ended in 1953, Korea remains one of the most potentially troublesome spots in the Far East, and the peace negotiations are still dragging on well over 30 years later, with no end in sight. The terrain can only be described as rugged, with mountains and valleys interspersed with swamps and paddy fields. Most of the roads, and therefore the routes for an armoured attack, are restricted by the terrain, while the weather is less than idyllic, with rain and low cloud for much of the year. In the event of hostilities, conventional fast mover air power would be hard to apply effectively; fast jets attacking up a valley under a low cloud base would have only one direction in which they could evade — upwards, which would effectively remove them from the fray as they lost visual contact with the ground, to say nothing of the difficulties of

attacking in the first place. The Warthog, with its ability to operate beneath the cloud base and turn within the confines of a narrow valley, would appear to be ideally suited to this scenario, and would be able to make full use of terrain masking tactics in a way that would not be possible in say the North German plain, which has little cover.

The role of the continental US-based units is the ability to reinforce local units at any trouble spot worldwide; in particular the two Tactical Air Command wings, the 354th and 23rd TFWs, are on standby, with the ANG and AFRes units providing back-up. Many deployments have been carried out to test this capability, a few of which have been particularly noteworthy. The first major overseas deployment by a US-based A-10A unit was undertaken early in 1979, when elements of the 354th TFW visited Hawaii in an exercise called 'Cope Elite'. The total distance of more than 4,000 miles was flown in two stages; Myrtle Beach to McClellan AFB just outside Sacramento, then across the Pacific, escorted by an EC-130 which acted as command, communications and navigational back-up. Close air support missions were flown over the Pohakuloa Training Area under the

Top:
Laden with external fuel tanks, a Wisconsin Air National Guard A-10A speeds down the Truax Field runway bound for West Germany, some 13 hours away.

Above:
This nice view shows the blade aerials beneath the rear fuselage of a 128th TFW aircraft. European 1 camouflage and low-vis markings are rather spoilt by the factory-fresh Pave Penny pod.

Above right:
The JAWS camouflage scheme, unofficially known as 'measles', is carried by this 57th FWW A-10A, which is armed with four practice bombs. *Frank Mormillo*

control of FACs, while their US Navy hosts at Barbers Point NAS provided 'MiGs' in the form of A-4 Skyhawks.

The largest overseas deployment of the ANG to date has been participation in 'Coronet Giant', when two ANG units, the 128th TFW from Truax Field, Wisconsin — more informally known as the 'Raggi Dieassm Ilitia' — linked up with the 174th TFW 'The Boys from Syracuse' from New York

108

tate and crossed the Atlantic to Germany to be
ased at Leipheim and Lechfeld in Bavaria
etween 28 April and 18 May 1984. Few oper-
tional problems were encountered, and the
European weather proved not to be the restricting
actor that had been feared.

The nearest the Warthog has come to being
nvolved in a shooting war was in 1983, when a
andful were deployed to the Caribbean during
ne invasion of Grenada, but were not used
perationally. The Warthog continues to patrol its
redictable beats, but every now and again it turns
p somewhere unexpected. The most recent
xample at the time of writing was the deployment
f 10 aircraft from the 91st and 510th TFS of the
1st TFW to Solenzara in Corsica, in November
986.

If only one variant of the Warthog has entered
ervice, this has been more than made up for by
ne variety of the paint schemes that have been
valuated over the years, which would take a full
hapter, if not a whole book, to describe in detail.
One of the main factors in survivability is the time
nat the aircraft is exposed to hostile fire; the less it
an be shot at, the fewer hits it is going to take, and
ne higher the survivability factor will be. The
nission as it is currently flown stresses a short
xposure time, and this can be reduced even more
the aircraft is made as difficult as possible to see,
s many surface-to-air systems depend upon visual
cquisition of the target. As a result, a tremendous
mount of time and effort, not to mention paint,
as gone into making the A-10A less visible.

The art of camouflage lies in making the object
o be disguised blend with its background. The
rouble is that the background is never constant,
nd no-one has yet come up with chameleon paint.

In the early days of the A-10A, the intended
nission profile involved a medium altitude
ansition to the target area, followed by an
xtended period of loiter at 5,000ft, and a series of
iving attacks. This meant that two threats had to
e considered: enemy counter-air and surface-to-
r defences. Camouflage in the Vietnam era was
or all practical purposes a throwback to World
Var 2, with a dark green/brown or grey/brown
pper surface, and a light coloured underside. The
op surface colours were only effective in masking
low flying aircraft; at medium altitudes they were
ot a lot of good. The original purpose was to
onceal aircraft on their airfields rather than in the
r, and it should be borne in mind that aircraft
pend far more time sitting on their airfields than
ley ever do in the air. The combination could be
ounterproductive in air combat, as a wingover
nowed a tempting flash of light coloured belly
hich could be seen for miles — to the extent that
became known as the 'Ivan thanks you very
uch' manoeuvre. The light underside offered a

measure of concealment against watchers on the
ground, but only as the aircraft passed overhead;
from head-on or the side it was useless, while if the
aircraft had a bright sky behind it, it always looked
black to the observer, regardless of what colour it
was painted.

A considerable amount of research into reduced
observables was carried out in the early 1970s, and
the result that emerged for air combat was grey.
The sky background varies an awful lot, from
cerulean blue through white cloud, grey mist, to
dark grey storm clouds, and a combination of greys
was found to be the most effective compromise. In
air combat a pilot most often viewed his opponent
against a sky background or a hazy horizon, while
a gunner on the ground always looked up at an
attack aircraft. The inference was obvious; the
same paint scheme would be best for both air
combat and ground attack.

The YA-10s both appeared in a light glossy grey,
with a matt black anti-reflection panel on the nose
in front of the cockpit. They carried standard — ie
full colour — USAF insignia, and engine pod
markings in red also. An all-over gunship grey was
the next colour tried, and this appeared on many
aircraft. The second of the pre-production batch,
No 73-1665, appeared in an odd pale grey mottle
achieved by using a thin white spray over a black
base, the white being spread unevenly. As flight
trials progressed, this machine became ever more
blotchy looking. Dark ghost grey was also used;
and at about this time, low-vis, all-black insignia
were introduced. This was followed by several
variations on a theme using two-tone grey, both
dark and light, with both disruptive and asymmet-
rical patterns. All-over light ghost grey was also
used on some A-10As. Tail codes and serials were

Above:
The sun reveals the wrinkly skin effect on this 354th TFW aircraft. Note that the 'hippy headband' does not extend right around the fin. *Fairchild*

most often in black but sometimes in white. Colourful Command and Unit insignia were often carried, the last sometimes in the form of a 'hippy headband' around the top of the fins. Aspect deception was sometimes used, in the form of a dummy canopy on the underside, in matt black with glossy patches to appear as highlights. A few schemes became standardised for a short while before being replaced.

The European 1 two-tone green scheme which we see today had its origins in the change in mission profile to a low level transit, and attacks using terrain masking. This meant that hostile fighters would be trying to locate the A-10A at very low level, where it needed to merge with the background. At the same time, attack pop-ups would be made wherever possible in a position that avoided skylining the A-10A, which immediately after would dive for the cover of the ground. The priority changed from being difficult to see against the sky to being difficult to see against the ground.

The JAWS exercises saw really freaky paint jobs as experiments were made to see which schemes gave the best results. Base colours of various greys, greens and even tan were used, with irregular blotches of four (or in some cases more) different colours. These odd-ball schemes became known as Jaws, although they were also referred to as lozenge, measles or even Afrika Korps revisited! Finally, with the European theatre of operations in mind, the A-10A emerged in the dull livery with which we are so familiar today, and which has proved to give the best results in what is really a no-win situation.

Sadly, it appears that the Warthog's days as a tank-buster are numbered. In 1985 the USAF launched an official request for information for a close air support/battlefield air interdiction (CAS/BAI) aircraft to replace the A-10A from about 1989. No funding is available for an entirely new design, and the choice has to be made from a type currently in the inventory, although it will have to be modified for the role. Four proposals

were made; Northrop F-20 Tigershark, which has since been pulled out of the running; an attack version of the General Dynamics F-16, which it has been rumoured will be based on the cranked-delta F-16F; McDonnell Douglas AV-8B Harrier II; and the Vought Strikefighter, which is a heavily rebuilt and modified Corsair II. Of these, the Corsair Strikefighter proposal is reported to be the favourite, for reasons which are probably fiscal as much as anything.

What then is to become of the A-10A? Many of the aircraft are brand-new by the standards of today, and may have as much as 20 years life in them. A USAF plan has been reported which proposes to cream off 100 of the newer machines to replace OA-37 Dragonflies in the FAC role, while the remainder will equip further AFRes and ANG units. This leaves two unanswered questions. The first is what massive technological leap has been made which will enable a fast mover to carry out the CAS role when the whole premise upon which the Warthog has been based said that it was not possible; while the second is, are they really going to send an aircraft which they have decided is no longer survivable in the modern battle zone, into the fray, as they will have to unless it is intended never to use the AFRes and ANG units? It can also be guaranteed that the United States Army will not like the idea, and considerable opposition will come from this quarter. Prophecy in modern air warfare is a perilous occupation, but it seems to the writer that there must be an excellent chance of the A-10A being reprieved, to soldier on for a further 15 years or so. Many Warthog drivers feel the same way, and they are probably better equipped than any to judge.

Data

hysical Data

ength: 53ft 4in
an: 57ft 6in
eight: 14ft 8in
ing area: 506sq ft
spect ratio: 6.53
npty weight: 21,519lb
ean take-off weight: 34,660lb
ax take-off weight: 50,000lb
ternal fuel (JP-4): 10,650lb
el fraction: 0.31
gines: 2×TF34-GE-100A unaugmented
rbofans
tal power static thrust: 18,130lb
aximum external load: 16,000lb
rdpoints: 11 (only 9 or 10 can be used)

erformance

ax speed at sea level: 390kt
ver exceed speed: 450kt
iling: 45,000ft
tial climb rate: 6,000ft/min
ke-off distance: 1,200-4,000ft
nding distance: 2,000ft
erational radius: 500nm
tal endurance: 4hr

adings, range given for no weapons except gun
ammunition, and with only 50% fuel, and
maximum all-up weight:
rust loading: 0.62-0.36lb/lb
ng loading: 58-99lb/sq ft

GAU-8/A Avenger 7-Barrel Gatling Type

Dimensions
Length of assembly: 19ft 10½in
Length of gun: 9ft 5½in
Maximum diameter: 3ft 3¾in
Calibre: 30mm

Weights
Feed system: 1,150lb
Mounting: 73lb
Gun: 620lb
Drive and controls: 120lb
Ammunition: 2,066lb
Total: 4,029lb

Feed system: double ended linkless
Drive system: dual hydraulic motors, 57.4W total
Rate of fire: 2,100 or 4,200 rounds/min
Time to rate: 0.55sec
Dispersion: 80% within 5mil
Average recoil force: 10,000lb
Barrel life: minimum 21,000 rounds
Reliability: Better than 20,000 rounds between
failures
Ammunition capacity: 1,175 or 1,350 rounds

GAU-8/A Ammunition

	PGU-14/B (API)	PGU-13/B (HEI)	PGU-15/B (TP)
Round length:	290mm	290mm	290mm
Round weight:	727g	662g	667g
Projectile weight:	425g	360g	365g
Propellant weight:	150-156g	148-156g	148-156g
HE weight:	nil	56g min	nil
Muzzle velocity (ft/sec):	3,225ft/sec	3,350ft/sec	3,340ft/sec

Units Operating the A-10A

Command	Unit	Base	Tail Code	Remarks
Tactical Air Command (TAC)	23rd TFW	England AFB, Louisiana	EL	
	354th TFW	Myrtle Beach AFB, South Carolina	MB	
	355th TTW	Davis-Monthan AFB, Arizona	DM	
	57th TTW	Nellis AFB, Nevada	WA	(was 57th FWW)
	TAWC	Eglin AFB, Florida	OT	(weapons testing)
Air Force Systems Command (AFSC)	Armament Div	Eglin AFB, Florida	AD	
	AFFTC	Edwards AFB, California	ED	(1983 only)
USAF Europe (USAFE)	81st TFW	RAF Bentwaters/Woodbridge, England	WR	
Pacific Air Forces (PACAF)	25th TFS	Suwon AB, South Korea	SU	(OS before 1985)
Alaskan Air Command	18th TFS	Eielson AFB, Alaska	AK	(part of 343rd TFW)
USAF Reserve (AFRes)	45th TFS	Grissom AFB, Indiana	IN	434th TFW
	917th TFG	Barksdale AFB, Louisiana	BD	(46th & 47th TFS)
	303rd TFS	Richards-Gebaur AFB, Missouri	KC	(442nd TFW)
	706th TFS	New Orleans NAS, Louisiana	NO	(926th TFG, 442nd TFW)
Air National Guard (ANG)	103rd TFG	Windsor Locks, Connecticut	CT	
	104th TFG	Westfield, Massachusetts	MA	
	128th TFW	Truax Field, Wisconsin	WI	
	174th TFW	Syracuse, New York	NY	
	175th TFG	Baltimore, Maryland	MD	